"As someone who has struggled with perfectionism and anxiety for most of my life, Kim Hyland's word̶ ̶ ̶ ̶ ̶breath and freedom to me. This i͏ ̶ ̶ ̶ ̶hear—not just once but many ti͏

    Holley Gerth  *Amazing*

"My friend Kim Hylan͏ ̶ ̶ ̶ ̶self-help book for women. She's ta̶ ̶ ̶ ̶ ̶ gospel and lit it up like a holy candle, shining it through our cracks and inviting us to not only acknowledge our imperfections but also take them to a perfect Christ and be made whole again. *An Imperfect Woman* is a convicting word in a culture that's lost any kind of righteous fear. It will woo you into the heart of a most loving Savior, and your life will never be the same."

    Emily T. Wierenga, author of *Atlas Girl*
    and founder of The Lulu Tree

"Like a well-trusted friend, Kim Hyland gets to the heart of the matter with grace and wisdom. With winsome stories and gospel-centered truth, Hyland's *An Imperfect Woman* is just the tome we need to kick perfectionism to the curb."

    Kristin Schell, recovering perfectionist and author
    of *The Turquoise Table: Finding Community*
    and Connection in Your Own Front Yard

"Jesus said, 'I have come that you might have life' (John 10:10), but many of us—myself included—hear that as 'I have come that you might be right.' There is a big difference between the two. Kim Hyland invites us to embrace the abundant life Jesus promised and to cast off our striving for, and idolatry of, rightness. Perfection is overrated and unattainable on our own. Get ready to let go of 'right' in exchange for 'life' as you turn the pages of this winsome book."

    Deidra Riggs, author of *ONE: Unity in a Divided World*

"Do you find you often have the best intentions but continuously come up short? Are you bone-weary of striving, yet don't truly know how to let your perfectionist tendencies go? Kim Hyland knows and understands your story and your struggle because they are her own. Lay down your good intentions, your striving, your spiritual perfectionism, and your shame, and let the sage wisdom and gentle teaching of *An Imperfect Woman* release you into wholeness, freedom, and gospel grace."

    Michelle DeRusha, author of *Katharina and Martin Luther: The*
    Radical Marriage of a Runaway Nun and a Renegade Monk

"In a world where we have become spiritually shortsighted, this book pulls everything on which we have been focusing into focus. Kim has written this book from a place of freedom, where once bondage existed. She helps us all see where we have believed lies of perfectionism and performance. I held on to every word Kim wrote with such grace and true humility. If there was ever a woman who could elaborate with grace-filled words, it is Kim Hyland."

September McCarthy, author of {*Why*} *Motherhood Matters* and founder/hostess of RaisingGenerationsToday.com

"In *An Imperfect Woman*, Kim creates a place where women can come—a place that's safe and welcoming for all. Through her own tender stories she unmasks the pretenses that bind us with perfectionism, comparison, condemnation, and more. In their stead, she offers the freedom that can only be found at the cross. Kim writes with true warmth and gentle honesty; the words on these pages are a retreat for the soul."

Denise J. Hughes, author of *Deeper Waters* and the Word Writers Bible study series

"With compassion and clarity, Kim Hyland brings a message of hope to every woman who wakes up each day striving to get it together and do better. Through the humility of the author's personal story, the depth of her teaching, and the boldness of a manifesto, *An Imperfect Woman* helps us understand and embrace what it means to walk in gospel freedom."

Ann Kroeker, writing coach and author of *The Contemplative Mom* and *Not So Fast*

"Kim Hyland writes with humility and passion as she shares rich, authentic stories that are a beautiful blend of theology, devotional, and memoir. *An Imperfect Woman* offers us a robust reminder of the gospel through her own stories of learning grace, battling perfectionism, and relenting to God's design for who we are created to be. It serves as a challenge to our own qualifications and pride, an encouragement to those who are exhausted by feeling they never measure up, and a song of praise for a God who both humbles and lifts up those whose hearts and lives are surrendered to him."

Alia Joy Hagenbach, (in)courage writer

AN *Imperfect* WOMAN

Letting Go of the Need
to Have It All Together

Kim Hyland

BakerBooks

a division of Baker Publishing Group
Grand Rapids, Michigan

Published by Baker Books
a division of Baker Publishing Group
PO Box 6287, Grand Rapids, MI 49516-6287
www.bakerbooks.com

Printed in the United States of America

Library of Congress Cataloging-in-Publication Data
Names: Hyland, Kim, author.
Title: An imperfect woman : letting go of the need to have it all together / Kim Hyland.
Description: Grand Rapids : Baker Books, 2018. | Includes bibliographical references.
Identifiers: LCCN 2017041924 | ISBN 9780801075162 (pbk.)
Subjects: LCSH: Christian women—Religious life. | Perfectionism (Personality trait)—Religious aspects—Christianity.
Classification: LCC BV4527 .H95 2018 | DDC 248.8/43—dc23
LC record available at https://lccn.loc.gov/2017041924

18 19 20 21 22 23 24   7 6 5 4 3 2

To
Jeff
Josh and Kim
Daniel, Hilary, and Amelia
Emily, Ethan, Elisha, and Ezra
Ben and Margaret
Joe
and
Sam

Your love and grace overwhelm me.

Contents

Contents

An *Imperfect* Woman's Manifesto

The woman in the front of the room held up a terra-cotta pot. It was perfect, without chips or cracks, smooth. Just like it should be.

"This is how I would like to be. Pretty perfect," she said. Then she picked up another pot. It had cracks and chips everywhere and had obviously been painstakingly glued back together. I could see where this was going.

That's nice, I thought.

"But *this* is how I actually am." She held up the cracked pot.

Yep. Knew it.

My cynicism was more a response of my exhaustion than meanness. I'd been at this gig too long and had given up. Proverbs 13:12 says, "Hope deferred makes the heart sick," and I was sick of heart. My hopes to create a life that would please God and fulfill me were crumbling. I couldn't try hard enough or go fast enough to outrun my inescapable imperfections and flaws and had resigned myself to failure. I didn't expect what would come next.

She placed a candle in each pot. As she lit the "perfect" pot, a warm glow emanated from the top. Then she lit the candle in the cracked pot and turned off the lights in the room.

Light streamed out from every crack, illuminating the entire pot. It was beautiful. In that moment, my paradigm began to shift. Maybe my despised imperfections had the potential to become something of beauty. Could they possibly be the very conduit of the grace, love, and light of God? For the first time in a long time, I had hope.

As I began to better understand and walk in God's grace, I experienced a freedom I'd never imagined, and my eyes were opened to so many of my peers who were still walking in bondage to performance and perfectionism. I wanted to break the chains and expose the lies that I saw all around me. That's the thing about freedom—it makes an abolitionist of those who've experienced it.

Not long after I discovered this newfound freedom, I was having dinner with a good friend, a woman who loves God wholeheartedly and has poured her life and God's Word into her family. She said that she felt she was ineligible to encourage others in their mothering because of her children's struggles and failures. Driving home, I was reflecting on our conversation, and I got angry.

I was angry at perfectionism. Angry at lies that deceive and rob us of our inheritance as daughters of the King and *make little of grace*. What is this lie we've swallowed that says until we get it together (whatever *together* is), we're not fit to advance truth and the kingdom of God? As I drove, in my head I began to compose An *Imperfect* Woman's Manifesto.

An *Imperfect* Woman's Manifesto

The Gospel's Proclamation

I will reject spiritual perfectionism and *embrace gospel grace*.

I will reject pride and *embrace humility*.

I will reject condemnation and *embrace forgiveness*.

The Gospel's Promise

I will reject anxiety and *embrace true peace*.

I will reject false security and *embrace God's sovereignty and provision*.

The Gospel's Price

I will reject idols posing as ideals and *embrace sacrifice, suffering, and hope*.

I will reject dressed-up lies and *embrace naked truth*.

I will reject safety and *embrace the battle*.

The Gospel's Power

I will reject comparison and *embrace my story*.

I will reject myopic, earthbound plans and *embrace grand, eternal destinies*.

PART 1

The Gospel's Proclamation

Eden's Redemption

two trees stand before me
one I know well
its fruit luscious, heady, and ripe
the scent of knowledge, vanity, pride

my ancestors knew it
their lineage sustained and appetites sated
with its fallow fruit and empty promises

the knowledge of good and evil
the hope of immortality
to be like God

the same old lie
its deceit as fresh as the day
why is man so simple?

fig leaves make pitiful clothes
my nakedness and shame refuse to be covered
scrambling, dropping, hiding
(a lot like those dreams of being naked in public)

but simpletons love their leaves
their futile efforts to mask weakness and failure
refusing to acknowledge their desperate need
refusing to accept

only blood can cover sin

footsteps come near
questions too
"why do you hide from my presence?"

accusations abound
excuses fly
everyone else must be at fault
to bear the blame would be a burden that would crush

I know the sentence
he did not lie when he said
"you shall surely die"

so why does he fashion clothes to cover my shame?
from what cloth do they come?
skins?

death has come
blood does cover
but it is not mine
this blood is from another

a foreshadow stretching long
across ages and time
from earth's creation . . . to Gethsemane . . . to this
     moment

the garden is not so far from here
its drama repeated in every mortal life
to listen to the deceiver
or to believe my maker

yes, the garden is near

but the verdict, it has changed
for my advocate spoke and took all my blame
his hands bear the scars of my heart's newfound
    healing

he invites me to walk
to taste of the other
this fruit not forbidden
but offered freely
"come and eat"
he says
"of the Tree of Life"

The Gospel, a Perfect Fit for Your Reality

*I will reject spiritual perfectionism
and embrace gospel grace.*

The Spirit of the Lord is upon me,
    because he has anointed me
    to proclaim good news to the poor.
He has sent me to proclaim liberty to the captives
    and recovering of sight to the blind,
    to set at liberty those who are oppressed,
to proclaim the year of the Lord's favor.

Jesus (Luke 4:18–19)

Amy Howard was my best friend in first grade. She lived close by, and I can still see the path to her house in my memory. Out the sliding back doors, across our postage-stamp townhouse lawn, through the gate, past the playground, up the hill, across the street, and I'd arrive. We would sing into hairbrush microphones in her basement as we dreamed up plans for our rock band. I don't remember if we had a name for our up-and-coming band, but I do remember our signature song! It was "Sugar Pie Honey Bunch" (aka "I Can't Help Myself" by The Four Tops), and it was going to make us famous.

Amy's mom was cool. She encouraged our dreams of fame and even joined our band practice on occasion. My fuzzy memories of her are all positive. That is until Amy told me her cool mom didn't believe in God. I was devastated.

If you don't believe in God, you go to hell. Period.

This was the first and most important fact in my nascent theological arsenal. I remember feeling a sense of panic that quickly turned into anxious efforts to fix this dreadful problem—a mental and emotional state I'd come to know well.

"She *has* to believe in God, Amy."

"Well, she doesn't," replied Amy passively.

"But she'll go to hell!"

"No, she won't!" This time not so passively.

And my pleading continued.

I don't have any memories of Amy or her cool, atheist, hell-bound mom after that. But I remember an overwhelming sense of helplessness and sorrow. I couldn't fix it.

A couple years later, I heard the gospel for the first time. The message truly was *good news* for my passionate, do-good, striving, seven-year-old soul. It was *great* news! I'd found the sure path to goodness, God, and heaven.

A Place of Power

Our salvation is a powerful moment in our lives—the most powerful. We receive this gift, the gospel of grace, that literally brings us to life and equips us to live every day for the rest of our lives. The gospel proclaims that as we humble our hearts, we receive forgiveness for our sins. As children of God, we're promised his sovereign care, provision, and peace.

While salvation is a free gift of God, the gospel calls us to a life of sacrifice—and even suffering—but always hope. Its truth becomes our standard, and we are equipped for the spiritual battle we've always fought anyway. The difference is now we are on the offense—and winning side.

The gospel comes with power! Its power is revealed through our stories and grand, eternal destinies designed by our Father for each one of us.

This gospel story of God's great love and grace through Jesus and its *proclamation, promise, price,* and *power* are at center stage when we first receive the gift of salvation. The gospel of grace has all our attention.

And our enemy Satan knows if we stay in that place of deep truth, dependence, and reliance on our Father—this deep awareness at the foot of the cross of his grace and our sinfulness, the forgiveness we receive, and the love exchange that takes place there, that place focused on God's grace—we will become a real threat in the spiritual battle. So he goes to task creating distractions, counterfeits, and whatever he can to get our eyes off grace.

My Story

I was raised in a churchgoing home by first-generation Christians. My father, a handsome Puerto Rican from Brooklyn, and my mother, a homecoming queen country girl from rural Pennsylvania, met in a laundromat in Washington, DC, in the late sixties. They quickly fell in love and married, and soon after, I joined them.

Dad had heard the gospel at the historic 1957 Billy Graham Crusade in New York City. He was twelve years old, and he went forward when Billy gave the altar call. Mom's encounter with the gospel was humbler but no less effective. She told stories of listening to her Pentecostal grandmother sing hymns on her porch in Hazard, Kentucky. Great-Grandma was sowing song-seeds of love and truth in the soil of my mother's young heart—seeds that would take root, grow, and in time supply fruit that would feed my faith.

Along with my parents, many loving and *imperfect* people molded my understanding of God and the Bible. But even in the midst of a Christian home, church involvement, private school, youth group, and Christian college, I came to equate *pleasing* with love. Of course, my misunderstanding carried over into my relationship with God. I would hide from him when I wasn't performing well and come to him only when I believed I was *worthy* of his approval and love.

I was distracted from grace, to say the least. I'd fallen for subtle yet destructive lies. My eyes were focused intently on my own beleaguered efforts to perfect myself. *Perfectionism* is defined as (1) any of various doctrines holding that religious, moral, social, or political perfection is attainable; (2) a personal standard, attitude, or philosophy that demands perfection and rejects anything less.[1] I'd forgotten the gospel message.

Being the fixer and planner that I was, I began strategizing for my future early on. I would do this thing right! I was ambitious through high school, graduating at sixteen and going off to college the following fall. I found my knight in shining armor, Jeff, and we were married when I was eighteen. I finished college at twenty, and our first son, Joshua, was born nine months later. My plans were coming together. I was determined to create a godly home and to continue to make myself worthy of God's love and blessings.

One child after another came rapid fire—a second boy, a girl, two more boys, and after deciding we were done having children, another boy four years later. As each child joined our family, I decided not only to carry the responsibility of my own sanctification but also to take charge of sanctifying my children's souls as well.

The years flew by, as they tend to do. I was living my dream, and I knew it. But why was it so hard? We homeschooled, Jeff was an elder, I taught Bible studies, I kept a *ridiculously* clean house for a family of eight. And I yelled a whole lot at my kids. I was a Bible-toting, churchgoing, song-singing, hard-striving young wife and mother.

For all of my striving, we were doing . . . *okay*. I was stressed out all the time, my oldest son and I argued constantly, and our second son was running away. But we were okay, because we homeschooled, my husband was an elder, I taught Bible studies, and the house was clean most of the time. And *Emily*.

Emily said, "Yes, ma'am," taught Bible studies to her little friends in the neighborhood, helped me all the time, was a leader and example among her peers, and loved Jesus wholeheartedly.

She also had nowhere to go with the reality of her sin. Emily had embraced the same striving, try-hard life as her mother and was a really "good" girl. When it came to my only daughter, I felt successful.

Until the day I walked into her room unexpected and discovered Emily was cutting. It looked like a cat had attacked her stomach. Had you told me that my sweet, little thirteen-year-old daughter was cutting, I would have said you were crazy. Emily said, "Yes, ma'am," taught Bible studies, and truly loved Jesus wholeheartedly! Cutting wasn't part of my plan.

We went on to discover that Emily was deeply depressed and had an eating disorder. My world crumbled. It crumbled not because I loved Em more than her brothers, but because I felt like she was the *one* I was getting it right with, and now I'd failed with her too. And I gave up. I kept going through the motions, but my heart wasn't in it. *How* could I work so stinking hard and still fail so profoundly as a mom?

The helplessness and lack of control I felt were paralyzing. As a mother, you will do anything to protect your children. But what do you do when their enemy is themselves? My mind was frantic, but every strategy and fix I could conceive came up to a dead end. I would lie in bed at night begging God to protect Emily from herself. Begging him to fix *us*. My heart was breaking. What I didn't know was that in my desperation God was breaking the back of perfectionism in my life. My life's greatest failure would become the means of my freedom.

In his wisdom, love, and mercy, God had begun to sabotage my strategies.

> I am the vine; you are the branches. Whoever abides in me and I in him, he it is that bears much fruit, for apart from me you can do nothing. (John 15:5)

The word translated "abide" in this verse is the Greek word *meno*. It means "to remain; not to depart; to continue. To remain as one; not to become another or different."[2] At the moment of salvation, we literally become *one* with Christ. I don't know that I think of myself as *that* integrated, that I am *one* with Christ and therefore I'm not to *become* another or different.

Our family lives on seven acres tucked into the side of a mountain. A couple years ago, my son Ben and I were out hiking. As we walked through our woods, I began to notice places where dead trees had fallen over and landed in the crook of a live tree and, after some years, had literally become a part of the living tree. It was fascinating to see these odd branches sticking out of what seemed like two trees, but on closer examination I could see how they'd actually *become one* as the tree that was alive grew around the dead tree.

That is a picture of us! Our spiritually dead lives have been incorporated into the living Christ just as the dead branches I saw became actual parts of the living tree. The difference is, unlike the dead branches, we are made alive and able to produce spiritual fruit. Like branches that can't survive without connection to the vine, we can't do anything apart from Jesus. The commentary of the *New Geneva Study Bible* describes our ongoing dependence this way: "The total inability of the unregenerate sinner makes saving grace absolutely necessary for the beginning, the development, and the completion of salvation."[3]

This passage is an undeniable affirmation of the gospel's relevance in our lives, not just at the moment of salvation but every single day! If we stay in relationship with God but don't *abide* in grace, we inevitably fall into spiritual perfectionism. A genuine love for God turns into performance-based striving leading to either pride or condemnation or, more likely, a miserable mix of both. When I'm doing well, I'm proud. When I fail, I feel condemned.

Relevant

Years ago I prayed that God would make the gospel relevant to my daily life. I embraced its truth, but in all honesty, I failed to see its relevance beyond a prayer I'd prayed when I was seven and something I was supposed to be telling others about. It seemed like Christianity 101, and I considered myself well into the 300-level courses. I genuinely loved Jesus, sought him daily, and yearned to obey his Word. My prayer was motivated by a desire to relieve my guilt for not sharing the gospel. It seemed like such an effort to tell others about him.

His answer surprised me. It still surprises me. *Every* day! What I'd hoped would be a renewed conviction for loving the lost instead became a profound realization of my own need for gospel grace every day.

The gospel—or *good news*—is God's perfection and righteousness given to us through the death and resurrection of Jesus. You probably already know that, but do you see how perfectly that news fits with your imperfection? Every single day!

In her remarkable book *Counsel from the Cross*, Christian author and psychologist Elyse Fitzpatrick warns that Scripture can become like Christian "white noise."[4] We acknowledge it but really don't notice it. It's like the hum of a fan running in the background of our spiritual lives. We need to turn up the fan, point it in our faces, and feel the power of its presence and truth as we take a close look at the gospel and its proclamations!

The crux of the gospel is this exchange: God's righteousness for our unrighteousness, his holiness for our sin, his perfection for our imperfection, his amazing grace for our lawlessness.

> For God has done what the law, weakened by the flesh, could not do. By sending his own Son in the likeness of sinful flesh and for

sin, he condemned sin in the flesh, in order that the righteous requirement of the law might be fulfilled in us, who walk not according to the flesh but according to the Spirit. (Rom. 8:3)

God's perfect law is a reflection of his perfect righteousness. It must be kept. Perfectly. The "righteous requirement of the law" must be fulfilled. The law of God is perfect, but I was born imperfect and flawed beyond hope and bear the fruit of the seed of sin. On my own I am helpless and hopeless to overcome sin and keep God's law, no matter how much I want to.

So in comes my hero, my Savior. He takes the punishment for my sin and gives me his righteous perfection. What a trade! "There is therefore now no condemnation for those who are in Christ Jesus" (Rom. 8:1). But why? "For the law of the Spirit of life has set you free in Christ Jesus from the law of sin and death" (v. 2).

What a beautiful title: *the law of the Spirit of life*. This is the law that set me free from *the law of sin and death* and the law *to* which I have been freed! I am now freely bound to this law of the Spirit of life. This is why the apostle Paul called himself a *bondservant* of Christ. A bondservant is one who has been freed, but by his own volition he chooses to bind himself to his master.

So then, brothers, we are debtors, not to the flesh, to live according to the flesh. (v. 12)

The *flesh* either rejects God's law or demands perfect obedience to the law walking in its own strength.

For if you live according to the flesh you will die, (v. 13a)

You will die, whether in arrogant sin and rebellion against God or in a self-determined pursuit of God, aka spiritual perfectionism. A life lived according to the flesh is marked by confidence in self.

> but if by the Spirit you put to death the deeds of the body, you will live. For all who are led by the Spirit of God are sons of God. For you did not receive the spirit of slavery to fall back into fear, (vv. 13b–15a)

Notice what emotion marks the spirit of slavery to the law of sin and death. It's fear.

> but you have received the Spirit of adoption as sons, by whom we cry, "Abba! Father!" (v. 15b)

Abba is the Jewish word for daddy. This is the image of a beloved daughter who cries out in humility and weakness, but in power too because of the strength of her daddy.

A proper understanding of the role of law and grace in our lives leads us to a proper response to the reality of the sin we are faced with daily, both our own and the sin of those around us. A *law*-informed response is marked by a discouraging and defeating progression: the delusion that we are capable of perfection on our own; denial of our imperfection; condemnation when we can no longer deny our imperfection; frustration, anger, and rebellion because we are faced with a hopeless task; and ultimately destruction, because we have no refuge from sin.

But a *grace*-informed response to our sin is marked by a path that leads us to Christ again and again: recognition of our failures and imperfection; conviction of the Spirit; repentance in response to his kindness; and ultimately restoration and a deeper intimacy with our Father, our Daddy, because of his love.

Too many women who are followers of Christ are living in the strength of the flesh and the spirit of slavery. They are fearful and impotent in their spiritual lives because of a flawed understanding of sin and who we are in Christ and with a death grip on the law for security.

The fruit of this kind of life is rotten. The denial of our absolute inability to keep God's law results in exhausting and futile efforts to attain spiritual perfection. We're reluctant to acknowledge our own sin, or we deal with sin harshly, condemning our loved ones and ourselves. When we put all hope in the law and flesh, we make Jesus's death on the cross to no effect. This is a crushing burden to bear.

I wonder how often the choice to reject faith in Christ or to settle for mediocrity is due to this burden and frustration with the inability to overcome sin in the flesh. How many women find themselves in a swirling vortex of confusion, condemnation, and destruction that feeds off itself and leads to the professed or passive abandonment of their faith?

It is vital for women to understand truth regarding the process of redemption and sanctification. Otherwise, at best we miss an incredible opportunity to walk in truth and grace. At worst we fall into rebellion against God, and by our example we lead others astray, teaching them to walk and put confidence in the flesh, which, according to Romans 8:5–8, is "death, . . . hostile to God," and "cannot please God."

> For we are the circumcision [we are the ones who have been chosen, marked, and set apart], who worship God in the Spirit, rejoice in Christ Jesus, and have no confidence in the flesh. (Phil. 3:3 NKJV)

We should not be surprised at how frequently we fail but rather that we walk at all in righteousness! The accuser of my soul wants to fix my focus on all my failures, flaws, insufficiencies, and imperfections. But the *lover of my soul* beckons me to look up to the cross, remember the reality of his perfection sacrificed for my imperfection, and embrace his grace.

> For if a law had been given that could give life, then righteousness would indeed be by the law. But the Scripture imprisoned everything under sin, so that the promise by faith in Jesus Christ might be given to those who believe.
>
> Now before faith came, we were held captive under the law, imprisoned until the coming faith would be revealed. So then, the law was our guardian until Christ came, in order that we might be justified by faith. But now that faith has come, we are no longer under a guardian, for in Christ Jesus you are all sons of God, through faith. (Gal. 3:21–26)

Through my ongoing struggles and failures, God has revealed to me the deep, deep relevance of the gospel in my everyday life. I choose each day to respond to my sin either with condemnation, hopelessness, and beleaguered efforts to perfect myself or in the light of the gospel, which purifies my heart and motives for obedience. When I remember grace, I am affirmed as *completely* accepted and loved by God because of Christ, and I respond in gratitude and trust. The very good news of the gospel arrives every morning and meets me right where I am. *It is a perfect fit.*

Before I began to embrace practically the grace found in the gospel each day, most of my mornings started out with big plans. But even after spending time praying and reading the Word, I'd be two feet outside my bedroom and everything would crumble as I was bombarded with my inescapable imperfection. Fussy children, unending to-do lists, emails, bills, and life's myriad challenges would upend my resolve in a moment to "do this day right."

Darn. I guess I'll try again tomorrow, I'd think. And I would trudge through my day.

But when I began to see the relevance of the gospel in my everyday life, I saw how it was a perfect fit for my reality. The gospel enables me to live in joy and freedom *here* with *these* people and in *these* circumstances. Nothing needs to change. *That* is good news!

Feeding Grace

Slowly, carefully, and so humbly, she lifted the cup to the young woman's lips.

I watched the caretaker and how she served the young woman, severely handicapped and bound to her wheelchair. The caretaker's beauty was radiant. Peace oozed out of her. She seemed to have true joy in her serving.

And now the generous servant held life to the chair-bound's lips. A remembrance of sacrifice, forgiveness, grace, and hope. An offering the weaker couldn't experience on her own. Someone needed to help her. She needed someone to feed her grace.

I wept, stifling sobs, as I witnessed this act of incomparable beauty. As long as I live, I will remember this image when I take communion. It was a picture of all the sacrament encompasses. The communion of strength and weakness, of grace and need, of lover and beloved. Body broken for broken body.

Later, I discovered that the caretaker was the young woman's mother. Who better to serve grace to her daughter? She was a picture of all I want to be as a woman who cares for my loved ones. Humble, careful, slow. Considerate of weakness, brokenness, and need. Strength that serves. Feeding grace.

And her beloved daughter? She was a picture of who I truly am! Helpless to save myself. In perpetual need of another's constant care. Dependent, loved, and secure because of the love and sacrifice of another.

QUESTIONS FOR REFLECTION

Spiritual perfectionism relies upon perfectly keeping the law, while the gospel is the good news of God's grace in our imperfection. In your day-to-day life, which of these do you tend toward?

What are the areas in your life in which you need to reject spiritual perfectionism and embrace the grace of the gospel?

What are some practical ways to "turn up the fan" so the gospel of grace is more than white noise in your spiritual life?

Why is there "no condemnation for those who are in Christ Jesus" (Rom. 8:1)?

According to Romans 8:13–15, what spirit have we not received? And what spirit have we received?

How much confidence should we put in our flesh, our own ability to achieve righteousness (Phil. 3:3)?

What was the intended role of the law until Christ came (Gal. 3:21–26)?

What are some ways you can demonstrate a "grace-informed" response to your sin?

Humility's Good Fruit

*I will reject pride
and embrace humility.*

Humble yourselves [with an attitude of repentance and insignificance] in the presence of the Lord, and He will exalt you [He will lift you up, He will give you purpose].

James 4:10 AMP

L ying in bed in the early morning, I find myself in a familiar place. The circumstances of my life all come to mind at once, demanding to know *exactly what* I plan to do this day to fix, reorder, and manage them. As fast as I can devise a strategy for one problem, here comes another, jumping up and down and crying, "What about me?! What are you going to do about *this* problem?" My mind races, even before my eyes have opened. I can feel my heart. It's heavy and beating hard. Everything else in my body desperately pleads for a little more sleep. An escape. But I know it's too late. My life's circumstances are lining up out the door, and there's no turning back. I open my eyes, take a deep breath, whisper a weak prayer on the exhale, and get up.

Deceived

The story of Adam and Eve is one of the first told in Sunday school. It elicits cartoon images of discreetly covered body parts (they're in a garden, so bushes usually do the trick), a myriad of happily coexisting animals, apples, and snakes. It's a familiar story, and like many familiar things, its meaning is easily lost and the story dismissed as elementary. But you'd be surprised how much Adam, Eve, and their garden home have to do with our twenty-first-century struggle with perfectionism. It's worth taking a closer look.

The Lord God planted a garden eastward in Eden, and there He put the man whom He had formed. And out of the ground the Lord God made every tree grow that is pleasant to the sight and good for food. The tree of life was also in the midst of the garden, and the tree of the knowledge of good and evil. (Gen. 2:8–9 NKJV)

Eden was a garden of beauty and sustenance. Everything in it was created to be cared for and enjoyed, with one exception.

Then the Lord God took the man and put him in the garden of Eden to tend and keep it. And the Lord God commanded the man, saying, "Of every tree of the garden you may freely eat; but of the tree of the knowledge of good and evil you shall not eat, for in the day that you eat of it you shall surely die." (vv. 15–17 NKJV)

After proclaiming this single prohibition, God declared that Adam shouldn't be alone, and he made woman. His creation was complete, and it was a paradise unequaled since. Adam and Eve had *perfection* in Eden. Most importantly, they were in a perfect relationship with God and each other. Until the serpent showed up.

Now the serpent was more cunning than any beast of the field which the Lord God had made. And he said to the woman, "Has God indeed said, 'You shall not eat of every tree of the garden'?"

And the woman said to the serpent, "We may eat the fruit of the trees of the garden; but of the fruit of the tree which is in the midst of the garden, God has said, 'You shall not eat it, nor shall you touch it, lest you die.'"

Then the serpent said to the woman, "You will not surely die. For God knows that in the day you eat of it your eyes will be opened, and you will be like God, knowing good and evil."

So when the woman saw that the tree was good for food, that
it was pleasant to the eyes, and a tree desirable to make one wise,
she took of its fruit and ate. She also gave to her husband with
her, and he ate. Then the eyes of both of them were opened,
and they knew that they were naked; and they sewed fig leaves
together and made themselves coverings. (Gen. 3:1–7 NKJV)

The cunning serpent planted a seed of doubt in Eve's mind
when he questioned God's command: "Has God indeed said,
'You shall not eat of every tree of the garden'?" Other versions
translate the serpent's question in Genesis 3:1 as "Did God
actually say . . . ?" (ESV) and "Can it really be that God has
said . . . ?" (AMP). The Message captures the slyness of the
serpent's challenge best: "Do I understand that God told you
not to eat from any tree in the garden?"

But God had made only *one* tree off-limits: "Of every tree of
the garden you may freely eat; but of the tree of the knowledge
of good and evil you shall not eat" (Gen. 2:16 NKJV). His love
for Adam and Eve was evidenced by his generosity, and it was
love that motivated his prohibition as well: "for in the day that
you eat of it you shall surely die" (v. 17).

The serpent was challenging God's goodness and love, and
Eve took the bait (3:2–3). But Eve's addition to God's rule,
"nor shall you touch it," reflects a subtle shift in her thinking.
She wasn't focused on God's generous provision but on his
prohibition. God had used words like *every* and *freely* when he
spoke to Adam. In her response to the serpent, Eve used neither.

The serpent quickly buried the seed of doubt with the dark
deceit of a lie: "You will not surely die." He directly contradicted
God's Word and cast further doubt on God's goodwill toward
Adam and Eve by suggesting that God was holding out on them.

In short, the serpent's temptation of Eve was, "God is not
enough. Take charge!" He deceived her by getting her eyes off

God's generous love and provision and focused instead on God's supposed insufficiency, as well as her own lack—not enough power (*you will be like God*) and not enough knowledge (*knowing good and evil*).

Eve doubted God, forgot his command, stopped trusting him, became proud, and ultimately disobeyed her loving Creator. She believed that if she ate the forbidden fruit, she'd have what she needed. But the truth is that Eve's disobedience cut her off from the very One who was more than enough and had created Eden, a place of perfection, for her and Adam to live, where every need would be met and every deepest desire satisfied.

Eve didn't think she was better than God. She didn't think she was more powerful than God. She didn't think she was smarter than God. Eve just believed the lie that she needed *more* than God. *He wasn't enough.* In her disbelief, she turned her head and heart to her own resources, ambitions, and abilities. And in her disobedience, Eve condemned herself and all her sons and daughters to a lifetime of *not enough*.

Scapegoats

Years ago, one of our younger boys complained, "If it weren't for Eve and that darn apple, we wouldn't be in this whole mess!" As he struggled with his own temptations (replace the "apple" with one of many boyhood pleasures), Eve was a convenient scapegoat. After correcting his common error of misidentification (calling the fruit an apple) and reminding him that Adam quickly followed suit, I asked if he thought he would have responded more wisely to the serpent's deception.

"Of course I would have!"

And I realized humility's lesson would have to wait for another day. There would no doubt be plenty of opportunities.

While I may not blame Eve for all of my and the world's woes, I find plenty of other scapegoats. They're as close as my imperfect family members, friends, church leaders, and the many anonymous people I encounter daily. There's even one in my mirror.

"If only _____ (fill in the blank), I would feel better, act better, love better, perform better," and so on. Take your pick. It's a subtle grasp at perfection, or at least my minimally tolerable level of imperfection, and it's motivated by pride.

Eve's cataclysmic sin wasn't eating a piece of fruit. It was disobedience. Her disobedience began with doubt, was motivated by discontent, and was sealed with pride as she turned her trust from her good God to herself.

Pride has many faces. We know it by its most obvious one, arrogance. But arrogance, fear, anxiety, busyness, harsh judgments, and indifference are just a few of the faces of pride. Pride also plays a main role in perfectionism.

Made for Eden

Imperfection has become a trend. With hashtags like #live authentic and books persuading us to lay down the elusive goal of perfection, we have felt the noose of perfectionism loosen from around our necks ever so slightly. We can breathe again, and we're learning to enjoy life *as is*. Some for the first time. It's wonderful!

Until we forget and find ourselves chasing a newer and better promise for soul satisfaction. Why is it so easy to slip back into perfectionism?

It is because we are *made* for Eden. Our hearts are forever longing to return to that place of perfection. That is why we are forever vulnerable to the promises of perfection that come in every color, shape, and size. When one doesn't satisfy, there are a million others that might. We embark on a futile yet relentless pursuit of our legitimate, God-given desire for Eden and its perfection, wondering why nothing ever quite satisfies our hearts. And perfectionism takes root.

Do you remember our definition of perfectionism in chapter 1: "a personal standard, attitude, or philosophy that demands perfection and rejects anything less"?[1] In light of what we've discovered so far, here's a working definition of perfectionism: a futile attempt to achieve perfection on our own; a demand for control of our lives now and on our terms; the original temptation.

Not Enough

All of advertising is built on the idea of *not enough*. There's something missing. *This* will make you happy, fix your problems, bring satisfaction. And it does. For a minute, maybe a day or two, even a week, if you're really lucky. Have you ever wondered why our *not enoughs* seem so insatiable?

Right now I'm sitting on a "new to us" couch. With a houseful of boys who tend to break couch frames with their wrestling, we've had only one truly new couch in almost three decades of family life. It's just not worth it to buy something brand new, so we keep our eyes open for like-new hand-me-downs.

Recently, I noticed the couch in our sunroom, the smallest and most popular room in the house, had seen better days. Maybe it was when my dad graciously suggested that putting a piece of plywood under the cushions might help give it more support. I guess he didn't find sitting with his knees up near his nose comfortable.

Since the room is so popular, I figured a sectional would probably be the best use of space. So I watched Craigslist and drooled over the *truly* new sectionals at Costco.

Earlier this week, my sister called and said they were getting a sleeper sofa for their daughter who'd just returned from college and had lost her room to a sibling. Did I want their old sectional? Perfect!

I went and picked it up the next day. After hauling the "knees in your nose" couch to the dump, we deposited the new-to-us sectional in the sunroom. It was a perfect fit! That evening, three of us stretched out on it while our granddaughter walked back and forth across the big *new* couch.

Today I spent a couple hours redecorating the room to match the color of the sectional.

It looks lovely. But it's not comfortable. So this afternoon I'm back online searching for another sectional.

My sectional is *not enough*. And that's not really a big deal. The big deal is when my *not enoughs* begin to rule my heart, define my identity, lay claim to my security, and take my eyes off the One who is enough.

The irony is that *not enough* is actually the truth. Nothing on this earth will fill my heart's cry for Eden. Everything in my being longs for that place of perfection—the place where all my needs are provided for, where I'm absolutely secure and loved, and where my heart's desires find fulfillment.

The problem with the *not enoughs* is how they can lure me into a futile search to fill my heart with things that will never satisfy it. That is pride at its most deceitful, because it's true: outside of Eden and on my own, there really is *not enough*.

Pride of Life

"Mom, you're the Christian self-help queen!" That was my adolescent son's conclusion as he looked at the titles lining my overflowing bookcase. He was right. I was determined to find *the* book that would tell me how to be the best wife and mother I could be. In other words, perfect.

I'll be the last to bash books written to encourage and guide women in their walk with Christ. A decade after my son's astute observation, my bookcase is still overflowing, and I've added half a dozen more. No, not books—bookcases! But every tool has its proper place and function. A hammer is great for pounding nails but doesn't work very well as a screwdriver. And no tool can *ever* replace the craftsman. Only he knows the design and end product and what tool to use when. Likewise, the best of men and women's wisdom can't ever replace that of our maker.

But what could have possibly been wrong with my desire to be a good wife and mom? There's no one I love more than my husband and children. Of course, I wanted to be my best for them! My desire was born from a very good place. But even a good desire can go bad.

> So when the woman saw that the tree was good for food, and that it was a delight to the eyes, and that the tree was to be desired to make one wise, she took of its fruit and ate. (Gen. 3:6)

Eve was tempted by good things: sustenance ("good for food"), beauty ("a delight to the eyes"), and wisdom ("to be desired to make one wise"). Who could fault her?

What we typically perceive as pride is actually its ugly fruit. The impulse of pride seems innocuous. It appears reasonable, even responsible. Pride begins with a tiny shift of the trajectory of my heart away from God as my source and the One to whom I owe all my allegiance. My heart is motivated by pride when I place my ultimate trust in something or someone other than Christ. Pride reflects an overblown estimation of my ability to manage my life and circumstances. It's delusional at best, rebellious at worst. Either way, it reflects a return to unbelief. The Bible calls this the *pride of life*.

> Do not love the world [of sin that opposes God and His precepts], nor the things that are in the world. If anyone loves the world, the love of the Father is not in him. For all that is in the world—the lust and sensual craving of the flesh and the lust and longing of the eyes and the boastful pride of life [pretentious confidence in one's resources or in the stability of earthly things]—these do not come from the Father, but are from the world. The world is passing away, and with it its lusts [the shameful pursuits and ungodly longings]; but the one who does the will of God and carries out His purposes lives forever. (1 John 2:15–17 AMP)

Pride of life reveals itself in as many ways as there are individuals. For me, it was family life. I was going to do it "right," and my pride and perfectionism just about strangled all the joy out of one of the greatest gifts of my life.

Perfectionism Paralysis

"That's not how you do it!" I said.

In hindsight, my son's tense face revealed his frustration and discouragement. But all I saw was stubbornness. I proceeded to show Josh *exactly* how to clean the kitchen counter.

"You wipe off the crumbs first. Then you spray the counter and scrub it. When you're done scrubbing, you rinse out the rag and wipe it again."

Josh didn't appear to be listening, which only made me angrier.

"Mom, do you really think there's only *one right way* to clean the kitchen counter?"

My knee-jerk response was *he's arguing again!* But something about his tone stopped me. In a moment of something close to humility, I realized it was an honest question.

Do I really believe there's only one right way to clean the kitchen counter?

I pondered a moment.

I do!

I was as incredulous as Josh was sincere. I really believed there was only one right way to clean the kitchen counter! And only one right way to clean the bathroom. And only one right way to dust. And only one right way to educate. And only one right way to discipline. And only one right way to do marriage, parenting, friendship . . . one, and *only* one, right way to live life. And it was up to me to find it.

What pride. What idiocy! What a crushing burden to bear.

Perfectionism is paralyzing. Many of my days were filled with frustration, anger, futility, and depression. "No matter how hard and fast and smart I work, it's *never* enough." The message in my head that eventually stuck was *I'm not enough*. And that was the same message I unwittingly conveyed to my family.

Perfectionism takes amoral things like clean kitchen counters and makes them the measure of morality, of *goodness*: I'm a *good* wife if my husband is happy. I'm a *good* mom if my kids are clean, mannerly, and well-behaved. I'm a *good* student if I rank in the top of my class, get into my first choice of colleges, and maintain a 4.0 GPA.

In a morally relativistic culture, good is easily replaced with successful, and the trap is set again: I'm a *successful* entrepreneur if I make at least six figures. I'm a *successful* blogger if my Instagram feed has five hundred, one thousand, ten thousand, one hundred thousand followers.

Humility 101

After Emily had been in counseling for a number of months, her counselor helped me see how my perfectionism not only robbed me of joy but was also crushing my kids. Emily had always been compliant, and my standards just kept increasing for her. I wanted her to be like me, but better. So I judged her harshly and applauded her wildly. Both were destructive.

Em and I have a lot in common, but there are many areas where we are different. Em is spontaneous, and I love routine. She's quick, thorough, and doesn't sweat the details. I am slow, methodical, and easily mired in minutiae. Em is deep; I am too, but the way we express ourselves is poles apart. Her uniqueness is what I love and appreciate so much about her now, but when she was young, it scared me. So I controlled her with expectations and rules. One of those had a lot to do with how she looked.

Our counselor encouraged me to let Emily express her individuality. She's supercreative, and I'd never given her the freedom to express her creativity in her style. Hypermodesty was all the rage in our conservative homeschool world, and I'd jumped on the bandwagon. Our counselor suggested that I not challenge Em on her clothing and appearance unless I *absolutely* couldn't tolerate her choice. This would be much harder than I expected. It was also some of the best counsel she ever gave me.

We were at a weekend homeschool event. Em was "expressing" her individuality all over the place. I'm not sure she even knew what she wanted to say; she'd been muzzled so long. As I watched other moms cast disapproving looks her way, my heart broke. I couldn't judge them for judging. They were acting just like I always had! But the shoe was on the other foot, and it fit so oppressively tight.

Everything in me wanted to plead, "You don't understand. She's actually getting better. This has been the hardest time of her life . . . of *my* life! If you only knew how dark our days and nights have been, you'd understand. *Please* don't judge my girl. I messed up. It's not her fault. I understand how you feel, but she's not the threat you think she is. We're trying so hard. We're going to be okay. I think. Please show us grace. Please encourage us. Please love us."

I was learning humility.

Humility Personified

God knew when he made us that we'd never find contentment outside of his perfection. Eden was forever lost to Adam and Eve when God sent them away, but he promised to restore his children one day to that perfect place. This time he'd do it through his own Son. Only Jesus can satisfy our hearts' longing for perfection. But it takes a humility that is willing to forsake our pride and its many manifestations.

Humility isn't a virtue that initially strikes us as bold and strong; rather, it evokes weakness, quiet, and even suffering. Humility may well involve all of these, but it is also empowering.

> Do nothing from selfishness or empty conceit, but with humility of mind regard one another as more important than yourselves; do not merely look out for your own personal interests, but also for the interests of others. (Phil. 2:3–4 NASB)

While we may readily acknowledge the vices of selfishness and conceit, we aren't as inclined to embrace the virtue of humility, especially when it requires us to regard others as more important than ourselves. It sounds so *self*-deprecating and totally goes against our *self*-made culture. When you're measured by how closely your life aligns with the images of perfection bombarding you daily, *self* becomes pretty important.

Popular concepts and words like *self*-confidence, *self*-esteem, and *self*-worth confirm our cultural preoccupation with *self*. We need a new paradigm for humility. Thankfully, we have one in Jesus.

> Have this attitude in yourselves which was also in Christ Jesus, who, although He existed in the form of God, did not regard equality with God a thing to be grasped, but emptied Himself, taking the form of a bond-servant, and being made in the likeness of men. Being found in appearance as a man, He humbled Himself by becoming obedient to the point of death, even death on a cross. (vv. 5–8 NASB)

Jesus knew who he was, but he didn't use that knowledge to his advantage. Rather, he used his place of strength and position for the sake of others by relinquishing it and becoming a man. As the Son of God, equal with his Father, he had the right to *be* served, but he chose to serve instead.

If that's all he had done, it would have been more than we deserved. Jesus could have come and demonstrated to us the right way to live and left it at that. But he knew we needed more than an example of good behavior. Jesus wanted to bring us "back to Eden" by restoring us to his Father. We needed a Savior to rescue us from sin and all its destruction in our lives. So in humility and love, Jesus submitted to history's greatest injustice when he humbled himself "by becoming obedient to the point of death, even death on a cross."

> For this reason also, God highly exalted Him, and bestowed on Him the name which is above every name, so that at the name of Jesus every knee will bow, of those who are in heaven and on earth and under the earth, and that every tongue will confess that Jesus Christ is Lord, to the glory of God the Father. (vv. 9–11 NASB)

Jesus's humility led to his exaltation by his Father. What appeared to the world as the ultimate place of weakness—the cross—became the greatest symbol of sacrifice, hope, and power. His willingness to humble himself saved us.

Humility is not for the faint of heart. It takes faith, but as followers of Jesus, it is our only option. Entrusting ourselves to an unseen God whose ways and thoughts are higher than ours[2] is impossible to do from a stance of proud self-reliance.

> "God opposes the proud, but gives grace to the humble." Submit yourselves therefore to God. Resist the devil, and he will flee from you. Draw near to God, and he will draw near to you. Cleanse your hands, you sinners, and purify your hearts, you double-minded. Be wretched and mourn and weep. Let your laughter be turned to mourning and your joy to gloom. Humble yourselves before the Lord, and he will exalt you. (James 4:6–10)

James's sober instructions to an already troubled and suffering church reflect how necessary humility is to following Jesus and living the life we are called to as Christians. It is a vital means of God's grace and power.

In the bestselling book *The Purpose Driven Life*, Pastor Rick Warren offers this insightful definition of humility: "Humility is not thinking less of yourself, but thinking of yourself less."[3] As we learn to walk in humility, not only will we not demand our own way, but we also won't beat ourselves up when we fail. A humble spirit just isn't thinking a lot about self. It's also saying, "Yes, Lord," with a submissive heart to God's sovereign will as he reveals it day by day through our circumstances.

Humility widens our view as it minimizes self and sets our trials in their place. It enables us not to think so much of ourselves and frees us to see God's blessings even in the midst of trials instead of being threatened or angered by difficulty. And the fruit of embracing humility is humility in response to those around us. Our behavior and relationships should be marked by this fruit.

Letting go of the ambitions, expectations, and standards my pride had erected hasn't been easy. The serpent's hiss is ever present, tempting me to doubt, become discontent, and believe the lie that God is *not enough*. Humility protects my heart and mind from deception.

My morning battle demands immediate solutions. While my temptation seems as far from Eden as my messy bedroom is from Paradise, it's the very same. Will I trust God and his promises, power, wisdom, and love, or will I proudly turn to my own resources to manage my life? Will I believe *he is enough*?

"But we have this treasure in jars of clay, to show that the surpassing power belongs to God and not to us" (2 Cor. 4:7). In his wise design, God made us fragile and with a constant need of him. He did this so we would know his love and power not only at salvation but in our day-to-day lives as well. Humbly embracing the reality of our weakness and his strength opens our hearts and paves the way for us to walk with our Father in the freedom and intimacy Christ bought for us.

QUESTIONS FOR REFLECTION

Where are you tempted to doubt God's goodness and/or power in your life?

What are the areas of discontentment in your life?

Where in your life does unbelief manifest most often?

What resources are you tempted to turn to? What "fruit" do you turn your heart and eyes to as the thing that will save you?

What are your *not enoughs*?

Do you struggle with perfectionism, defined as "a personal standard, attitude, or philosophy that demands perfection and rejects anything less"?[4]

How about when it's defined this way: a futile attempt to achieve perfection on our own; a demand for control of our lives now and on our terms; the original temptation?

How invested are you in our culture's concept of *self*?

Where in your day-to-day life does Christ's example of humility motivate you to humble yourself? What does that look like in practice?

Guilty? Yes. Condemned? No Way!

*I will reject condemnation
and embrace forgiveness.*

Therefore, as one trespass led to condemnation for all men, so one act of righteousness leads to justification and life for all men. For as by the one man's disobedience the many were made sinners, so by the one man's obedience the many will be made righteous.

Romans 5:18–19

Rage. That's really the only word to describe it. I would try and try and try to stay calm. Until I'd blow. Perfectionism was a ruthless master and always impossible to satisfy with five kids eight years old and younger. Sadly, my beloved children were the undeserving target of my frustration and anger. As I yelled and screamed, they would slink away if possible or, worse, sit frozen and wide-eyed as their mama flipped out.

The guilt was unbearable. I would die for my kids. Every day was spent caring for their physical, emotional, and spiritual needs. My inner dialogue went something like this: *How could I be so harsh and mean? What is it in me that makes me flip out like that? For all my desire to be a good mother, I am a terrible person.*

For years, I read book after book on every aspect of the Christian life—being a godly woman, wife, mother, neighbor, and so on. Sometimes I was encouraged, although it was usually short-lived. The rest of the time I felt frustrated. They were wonderful ideals, and many (though not all) contained very biblical principles. They just always seemed so out of reach.

These books had become an end in themselves instead of a means to an end. And that was the problem. Rather than being a means of instruction and encouragement, they became an unreachable standard of performance. And as I tried so hard to live up to a constantly changing standard of perfection, I forgot my *true end* as a wife and mom: becoming a woman of peace who *both* enjoyed and reflected the love and grace of God to her family.

> There is therefore now no condemnation for those who are in Christ Jesus. For the law of the Spirit of life has set you free in Christ Jesus from the law of sin and death. (Rom. 8:1–2)

In hindsight, I see how I was trying to achieve these godly ideals in my own strength and not by the power of God's Spirit in me. As someone "in Christ Jesus," I'd been set free, but I was living as if I was still bound to "the law of sin and death" rather than in the freedom of "the law of the Spirit of life" in Christ Jesus. This freedom was the very thing that could equip me to implement the godly ideals I was studying.

I remember feeling immense relief when I stumbled upon Paul's explanation of his own struggle with sin in Romans 7:

> For we know that the law is spiritual, but I am of the flesh, sold under sin. For I do not understand my own actions. For I do not do what I want, but I do the very thing I hate. Now if I do what I do not want, I agree with the law, that it is good. So now it is no longer I who do it, but sin that dwells within me. For I know that nothing good dwells in me, that is, in my flesh. For I have the desire to do what is right, but not the ability to carry it out. For I do not do the good I want, but the evil I do not want is what I keep on doing. Now if I do what I do not want, it is no longer I who do it, but sin that dwells within me.
>
> So I find it to be a law that when I want to do right, evil lies close at hand. For I delight in the law of God, in my inner being, but I see in my members another law waging war against the law of my mind and making me captive to the law of sin that dwells in my members. Wretched man that I am! Who will deliver me from this body of death? Thanks be to God through Jesus Christ our Lord! So then, I myself serve the law of God with my mind, but with my flesh I serve the law of sin. (vv. 14–25)

"For I have the desire to do what is right, but not the ability to carry it out." Exactly! If the apostle Paul, author of over half the New Testament, wrestled with sin, maybe there was hope for me. Where had he been all my life?!

My Day in Court

Paul's declaration of freedom comes right on the heels of his confession. In Romans 7, Paul defines his predicament, then in Romans 8 he declares the glorious consequence of our salvation. Let's read it again:

> There is therefore now no condemnation for those who are in Christ Jesus. For the law of the Spirit of life has set you free in Christ Jesus from the law of sin and death. (vv. 1–2)

Romans 8:1 is a familiar verse to most Christians. It's often quoted when a Christian expresses feelings of guilt. I heard it when I shared with others my struggle with rage toward my children. "But you shouldn't feel guilty. There's no condemnation for those who are in Christ Jesus." These words are offered as comfort to our consciences. They purport to be the key to our release from the prison of guilt. But our cultural emphasis on emotions and feelings has skewed our understanding of sin, guilt, and condemnation.

It's true! There is no condemnation for those who are in Christ Jesus. But Paul isn't talking about emotions. His declaration isn't an attempt to assuage our guilty consciences. Paul is using legal terminology. He's painting the scene of a courtroom.

He stands *guilty* before a righteous judge. That's why he's so desperate. "Wretched man that I am! Who will deliver me from this body of death?" Paul immediately answers his own question: "Thanks be to God through Jesus Christ our Lord!" The word that is translated "through" is a preposition denoting the channel of an act. The act is Paul's deliverance through salvation, and it is *through* Jesus the channel. Paul is deeply aware of his guilt. But even though he *is* guilty, he is *not* condemned!

This is an incredibly important distinction. When I sin, I am *guilty* of that sin. The emotion of guilt is very appropriate. But that's not the end of the story. Guilty? Yes. Condemned? No way!

Our enemy Satan wants us to believe the opposite and say, "Guilty? No! I volunteer in the nursery at church. I work hard. I'm nice to the neighbors. I lead Bible studies. I sacrifice for my family." He knows that if we refuse to acknowledge the guilt of our sin, we will never be free from it.

But if we won't rebelliously deny our guilt, Satan takes another tactic. "Condemned? Yes. I'm alone in the courtroom. I have no advocate. No matter how hard I try, I can't be good enough. I'm guilty as charged and condemned without hope." This kind of hopelessness can keep us chasing our tails in futility for years. I know.

I also know that I'm not alone in this. We've attended the conferences, read the books, and done the studies, yet so often the fruit of our lives doesn't demonstrate the knowledge we've gained. Like many Christians, I relied on the law and my own strength to live a life that would be pleasing to God. *Thank God it didn't work!* It came crashing down and broke me in a way that at the time felt beyond redemption. But that was exactly what freed me to see I was still living like a slave and to begin living in the freedom that Christ bought for me through *his* perfection, not mine. My futile efforts to "do the good I want" and my consistency in doing "the evil I do not want" were the very things that brought me face-to-face with grace.

Grace's Backstory

Grace is popular. After decades of performance, legalism, and striving, it once again has center stage on many evangelical platforms. As someone who internalized the *try hard* life in my relationship with God, I'm thankful we've "rediscovered" grace!

But grace has a backstory. It's not a story that's told one time; it's repeated every day of our lives. It involves our sin and guilt, the Holy Spirit's conviction, genuine repentance, and forgiveness. Without these characters, the story is incomplete at best. At worst it's a lie.

The Christian church and its extremes have aptly been compared to a drunken man mounting a horse. He climbs up one side just to fall off the other. In our long-overdue embrace of grace, have we denied the truth of God's righteous law, his wrath toward sin, and judgment? Have we glossed over the sober Scriptures that warn us by naming who *won't* inherit his kingdom of grace?

I've listened to many of my children's generation decry legalism as they flirt with sin, all in the name of "grace." Partying on Friday, repenting on Saturday, and worshiping on Sunday with little to no acknowledgment of the impending and collective consequences of their Friday night forays.

Does God forgive on Saturday and welcome on Sunday? Absolutely! Every time. But do forgiveness and grace remove the *consequences* of Friday night's sin?

> Do not be deceived, God is not mocked [He will not allow Himself to be ridiculed, nor treated with contempt nor allow His precepts to be scornfully set aside]; for whatever a man sows, this and this only is what he will reap. For the one who sows to his flesh [his sinful capacity, his worldliness, his disgraceful impulses] will reap from the flesh ruin and destruction, but the

one who sows to the Spirit will from the Spirit reap eternal life. (Gal. 6:7–8 AMP)

We reap what we sow. Would we really want it any other way? As hard as our hearts might be toward God when we rebel against him and his precepts, what kind of world would it be if we expected good to come from evil, even our own? Or if we had no hope that choosing good over evil would be rewarded? Far from legalism, the cause-and-effect consequences of good and evil are *manifestations* of grace.

Legalism is the mistaken belief that our adherence to the law will save us. Acknowledging the truth of God's law and sin and judgment is not legalism, just as grace is not the *absence* of the law and sin and judgment. Knowledge of the law, sin, and judgment is what makes grace so glorious!

We break the perfect law of God every time we sin. We're absolutely guilty and would stand utterly condemned before a righteous judge. But God

> so loved the world, that he gave his only Son, that whoever believes in him should not perish but have eternal life. For God did not send his Son into the world to condemn the world, but in order that the world might be saved through him. Whoever believes in him is not condemned, but whoever does not believe is condemned already, because he has not believed in the name of the only Son of God. (John 3:16–18)

Jesus came to save us, not condemn us! Just as the sun chases away the night, God's amazing grace shines on and reveals our sin and guilt, drawing us to the warmth of forgiveness and love. We must continue to acknowledge and deal with the reality of sin if we desire to know grace.

I went to Mass this morning. I don't normally attend Mass on a weekday morning. In fact, I don't normally attend Mass at all. I'm not Catholic, but I have a deep appreciation for the historical church and Roman Catholicism's role in that story. Today is Ash Wednesday, and I wanted to start the Lenten season in church.

So did a lot of other people.

The large sanctuary was filled with people standing in back and overflowing into the vestibule. As I sat waiting for the service to begin, I couldn't help but think about how the reality of our mortality inevitably draws us to the hope of redemption from our sins and salvation from their just consequences. Based on the size of the crowd, it appeared I was not the only one looking for a reminder of this redemption. As I left with ashes in the form of a cross on my forehead, I was even more convinced of how release from the chains of sin must be preceded by *acknowledging* the chains that bind me and make me sin's slave.

The next forty days of Lent will escort me to the bloody cross. There the metal of my chains transforms to nails, as Jesus takes on my sin and punishment. My guilt is transferred to him, and he is condemned as he fulfills "the righteous requirement of the law."

> For God has done what the law, weakened by the flesh, could not do. By sending his own Son in the likeness of sinful flesh and for sin, he condemned sin in the flesh, in order that the righteous requirement of the law might be fulfilled in us, who walk not according to the flesh but according to the Spirit. (Rom. 8:3–4)

Through his sacrifice, Christ "condemned sin"! The story continues and leads me to the empty tomb where he overcame death, and I receive the sure hope of eternal life.

The Greek word translated "condemnation" in Romans 8:1 is *katakrima*, which means a damnatory sentence.[1] Condemnation is the *state* of being condemned. Often, we confuse condemnation with guilt and look at both condemnation and guilt as feelings or emotions rather than as states or conditions. The problem with this is that we are confused about our state before God our judge.

We have been found guilty of sin. Period. But because Christ took our punishment, we are not condemned. When we think of guilt and condemnation in terms of our emotions rather than in terms of our state before a holy and righteous judge, our response is flawed. Our emotions aren't irrelevant, but they're also not fail proof. We need to evaluate them and see if they align with truth. In this case, they need to emanate from the truth of salvation and our acquittal before God.

The law of sin and death is the operative power of sin—how sin works in our lives. *The law of the Spirit of life in Christ Jesus* is God's operative power—the power by which he operates. God does not operate by the law of sin and death. But Satan wants us to believe he does, because the law of the Spirit of life in Christ Jesus reveals God's love.

If there is anything the enemy of our souls wants to keep us ignorant of from day to day, it is the knowledge of and intimacy with the lover of our souls. Satan is happy for us to continue trying to live and function under the law of sin and death, because he knows that if we do, we will spend our lives either proud and deluded or defeated and believing we are condemned. This is why the gospel message is *good* news! It reveals God's love every single day, not in the *absence* of sin but in the *face* of our sin.

Two Sons "in Law"

The parable of the prodigal son in Luke 15:11–32 illustrates these two laws at work. Initially, both sons demonstrate their bondage to the law of sin and death. The son who rebels against his father, and thereby "the righteous requirement of the law" (Rom. 8:4), is eventually brought to reality by the consequences of his sin. Acknowledging the truth of his guilt, he knows he is no longer worthy to be a son. As a condemned man, he drags himself home in the hope of receiving just enough mercy to be deemed a servant in his righteous father's household.

The older brother, a self-righteous "keeper" of the law, denies his guilt. He believes he is worthy of his father's love because of his own righteousness. His pride is revealed by his anger when his father shows the younger brother not only mercy but also grace—unmerited favor—and welcomes his penitent son not as a servant but as a beloved child.

Living by the law, whether in rebellion or self-righteousness, separated both sons from the love and grace of their father. While the dutiful brother stayed home and worked hard, he didn't truly know his father's love since he believed it was earned by his faithful service. It's ironic that the son who comes to be set free from the law of sin and death by the law of the Spirit of life is the son whose behavior appeared to be the worst.

The older brother's denial of his sin blinded him to his need for the same grace being extended to his sibling. Humility, confession, and repentance brought the rebellious son back into a grace-filled relationship with his father—a relationship that his older brother had yet to experience.

> If we say we have no sin, we deceive ourselves, and the truth is not in us. If we confess our sins, he is faithful and just to forgive us our sins and to cleanse us from all unrighteousness. If we say we have not sinned, we make him a liar, and his word is not in us. (1 John 1:8–10)

While 1 John 1:9 is often quoted in reference to our initial repentance from sin at salvation, in the context of this passage, the apostle John is speaking of our daily walk with God. "It is an inescapable reality that believers sin; the remedy for sin—confession, and cleansing by the blood of Jesus—is God's continuing irrevocable gift to believers."[2]

Confession is not a onetime deal. Every day I stumble. As my relationship with God grows deeper, I become more and more aware of my sin. While justified by the blood of Jesus, I am utterly unlike him in his perfect righteousness. To deny my sin and guilt is to deny the truth of the gospel. To ignore my need for confession and forgiveness is to deny my daily need for his forgiveness and grace. Confession and repentance are how I avoid the error of either brother, rebellion or self-righteousness, and stay fiercely dependent on the love of the Father.

The Power of Confession

> Therefore, confess your sins to one another and pray for one another, that you may be healed. The prayer of a righteous person has great power as it is working. (James 5:16)

I read the words from James 5 with trepidatious hope. I'd prayed and prayed for God to give me control over my outbursts. While I confessed my sin to him privately, I hid my shame from everyone else. Maybe if I confessed to someone else and prayed with them, I would overcome the sin that seemed so insurmountable in my private life. It was worth a try.

Each time I lost it with the kids, I'd humbly pick up the phone and call my good friend Stephanie. As the mom of a passel of young kids herself, she could empathize, but empathy wasn't the focus of these conversations. Steph would listen as I confessed, and then we'd pray together. It was very natural, one friend reaching out to another for help. The difference was my intention and the hope that by confessing my sin to and praying with another member of Christ's body, I would overcome it.

It was hard at first. Who wants to tell someone when they've succumbed to temptation and sinned? But those calls quickly became a place of refuge from the seesaw of denial and condemnation. Was I guilty? Yes. Was I condemned? No way! Confessing to a trusted friend and praying together for forgiveness and healing became the means to overcoming my rage. My self-control gradually increased, and the incidents became less frequent. As I experienced God's tangible grace and forgiveness again and again through fellowship with his body, the accumulated weight of shame slid off my back. Confession was a powerful means of grace in my life.

> Search me, O God, and know my heart!
> Try me and know my thoughts!
> And see if there be any grievous way in me,
> and lead me in the way everlasting! (Ps. 139:23–24)

David asked *God* to search his heart and mind. He did not want to hide from his sin, and he didn't trust his own introspection. He asked the One who sees everything to search every dark corner of his heart and expose the sin he found. Perhaps this is why God said David was a man after his own heart. David hated sin and loved righteousness and was willing to humble himself and accept God's loving correction.

This is the kind of humility before God that avails us of the potential to tell the backstory of grace, the gospel, every day. Asking God to point out my sin; allowing the conviction of his Spirit to go deep into my heart and mind; confessing, repenting, and receiving his forgiveness; and experiencing his love and grace once again—all these combine to draw me closer to his heart.

Day by Day

How does all this knowledge affect my daily life practically? It equips me to challenge my emotion of guilt and to determine whether it emanates from truth or a lie. Perfectionism can lead us to assign morality to amoral things. For example, feelings of guilt because I am not keeping my house clean enough, exercising enough, volunteering enough, or *doing* enough are *false* guilt. I have not sinned by failing to achieve some contrived standard in these areas, and I am not guilty!

On the other hand, when I feel guilty because I have yelled at my kids, gossiped, complained, lied, and so on, my emotion of guilt is emanating from truth. I am guilty and in need of forgiveness. I may be tempted to deny my guilt and succumb to the lie: *Guilty? No.* Or I may hide in shame, forgetting the remedy God has lovingly given me: *Condemned? Yes.*

Shame emanates from condemnation that comes from the law of sin and death. If my state before God was just about my obedience, my performance, my deeds, my sin, my own attempts at righteousness, there's no question I would stand guilty. It would be hopeless. When I believe the lie of condemnation instead of remembering God's grace through the law of the Spirit of life in Christ Jesus, my heart grows dull, my eyes blind, and my ears deaf to my Father's love.

But when I reject condemnation, humble myself, and confess my sin, I experience anew my Father's forgiveness and love. Repentance that leads to forgiveness not only positions me to receive God's love but is also a place of power. The blood of Christ covers my sin and gives me the power to overcome.

Confession and repentance don't benefit only me. Because they keep me cognizant of the grace I've been shown, I'm able to respond to the sin of others with humility and grace. Sinners are no longer "other" than me. When I respond to my own sin according to the law of sin and death, I respond to the sin of others in the same way, and by my example I perpetuate a lie. But when I respond in truth according to the law of the Spirit of life in Christ Jesus, I proclaim the gospel.

Between the Once upon a Time and Happily Ever After

Story is deeply ingrained in us, as if it's part of our design. We like stories—stories with a happy ending, that is. But our stories aren't over yet. A young friend complained to me, "Christians are obsessed with stories that are finished. We tell the testimonies of people whose sin is in the past. It's as if their lives have been perfect ever since they decided to follow Jesus. What about the people who are still struggling? Why don't we hear their stories?" I understood. For years, I saw the women who "had it together" spiritually and thought the objective was to become like them. It's no mystery why so many followers of Jesus give up or trudge along defeated. When we don't expect to encounter temptation and sin along the journey, we are unprepared to navigate it. We give up and embrace its sin or bear its burden.

We tend to believe that the only stories worth telling are the ones that are wrapped up with a big red bow and a happily ever after. But the nature of sin and our battle with it belies that fantasy. When it comes to our justification and perfection in Christ, we live a *now and not yet* story. It's called sanctification, and it can be pretty messy.

Emily shared with me how during her struggle with cutting and depression, she began keeping a *good* list, a written list of all the good things in her life. Her intentional focus on the ways she saw God's grace and love in the midst of her battle kept her from sinking in the overwhelm of her present circumstances and gave her hope and strength for the fight. In hindsight, she recognized that she was practicing obedience.

> Finally, brothers, whatever is true, whatever is honorable, whatever is just, whatever is pure, whatever is lovely, whatever is commendable, if there is any excellence, if there is anything worthy of praise, think about these things. (Phil. 4:8)

Later, as she battled her eating disorder, she did it hand in hand with God, experiencing his grace, forgiveness, and strength as she struggled. The summer before Emily's senior year of high school, she was attending an acting conservatory in New York for six weeks. Her eating disorder was aggravated by the fact that she was on a tight food budget and had numerous expenses. It was the height of her struggle. It was also when she shared the gospel with a number of friends, some of whom made a decision to follow Christ.

To many Christians, that's a seemingly contradictory set of events. At one time, it would have seemed that way to me as well. It can be easy to forget that the One we follow is the One who built his church on a three-time traitor (Peter) and who chose a self-righteous murderer (Paul) to proclaim his good news to the Gentile world. But John tells us:

> My little children, I am writing these things to you so that you may not sin. But if anyone does sin, we have an advocate with the Father, Jesus Christ the righteous. He is the propitiation for our sins, and not for ours only but also for the sins of the whole world. (1 John 2:1–2)

Far from promoting a license to sin, John is reminding believers of the grace of forgiveness. He then goes on to speak of the standard of righteousness:

And by this we know that we have come to know him, if we keep his commandments. Whoever says "I know him" but does not keep his commandments is a liar, and the truth is not in him, but whoever keeps his word, in him truly the love of God is perfected. By this we may know that we are in him: whoever says he abides in him ought to walk in the same way in which he walked. (vv. 3–6)

John knows we are believers who wrestle with sin even as we walk in righteousness. Guilty? When we sin, yes. Condemned? Because of the glorious grace of the gospel and our good Father's persevering love and generous forgiveness, no way!

QUESTIONS FOR REFLECTION

Do you find comfort in Paul's confession in Romans 7? How so?

Are you more prone to believe the lie "Guilty? No" or "Condemned? Yes"? Explain.

Which side of grace do you tend to fall off of, the *try hard* life or denial of God's righteous standard?

How does the principle of sowing and reaping motivate you?

How do you see unbelievers around you looking for the hope of redemption?

Do you relate more to the rebellious prodigal son or his self-righteous older brother? Explain.

Are asking God to search your heart and confessing your sins regular parts of your life in Christ? If not, how could you make them so?

How have you experienced the power of confession and forgiveness?

How is God's grace showing up in your *now and not yet* story?

PART 2

The Gospel's Promise

Draw Near

fret not yourself
the multitude of your faults
are well known

don't try to hide them
tiresome efforts are in vain
their stench gives them away

strive no more
their stain goes deep
penetrating your soul

bow down low
look up high
here, your blessed recourse

gaze into his eyes
full of lover's longing
seeing only grace

feel his arms
reaching out to hold
the embrace of forgiveness

know perfect love
not earned, not bought
but received in faith

and rest

That Peace

I will reject anxiety
and embrace true peace.

When peace, like a river, attendeth my way,
When sorrows like sea billows roll;
Whatever my lot, Thou hast taught me to say,
It is well, it is well, with my soul.

> Horatio G. Spafford,
> "It Is Well with My Soul"

I was on my phone until almost 3:00 a.m. last night. I know better than to start checking on things in my own online world, much less the world at large, right before I go to sleep, but I gave in. Just for a minute. Yeah, right.

The day had been another one crammed full of bad news, with deadly shootings stacking up before we could catch our breath. I carried the frightening images, passionate words, desperate questions, and heavy heart all day. It's hard to look away from a culture in crisis, especially when its bloody wounds are live streaming and we can take it to bed with us. This morning the day-old sorrow feels fresh, and I'm banking on God's *new mercies* in the chaos of our world.

Anxiety about our world. Anxiety about my future, my health, my relationships, my kids, my weight, my house, and the dust on my furniture.

From the meaningful to the meaningless, latent anxieties crouch at the borders of my mind like squatters trying to lay claim. As soon as I turn my back, they begin to encroach. Some have infiltrated and set up tents. Others have built more permanent dwellings and behave like rightful owners of my mental and emotional landscape.

The first step toward evicting these squatters is to acknowledge them, but I really don't want to be bothered by anxiety. As I sit with my coffee and planner each morning, anxiety is not on the agenda. Sure, it may show up, but I do all I can to avoid it. Like the kid who puts her fingers in her ears and taunts, "Nah, nah, nah . . . I can't hearrrr you," I'm tempted to think ignoring my fear will make it disappear. But the reality is that when I refuse to address anxiety, I surrender ground. Anxiety thrives in the darkness of denial. But when I face anxiety with the light of truth, it runs.

Vulnerable

I'm sitting on my front porch. It's my outdoor office and keeps me "out of sight and out of mind" just long enough in our busy home to get some uninterrupted writing done. It's quiet except for the tractor mowing next door. Our dog, Pete, is keeping me company lying next to me. It's a muggy July morning and already in the eighties, but the shade and my glass of lemon water are keeping me cool. And there's a breeze blowing up the mountain. It is a peaceful morning, but there's no guarantee my day will proceed as it began.

Two weeks ago today, we were on vacation when we received a call from our daughter-in-law. Through choked tears she told us our son Daniel had been in a car accident and was taken by ambulance to the ER. His lung had collapsed, and he spent the weekend in the hospital. Photos of his totaled car told us how much worse the accident could have been.

A week and a half ago, the Istanbul airport was attacked by terrorists, and over two hundred people died. Our son Ben was in that same airport on layovers just two months ago traveling to and from Uganda. He's home safe now, but my thoughts are pulled to the what-ifs. What if the terrorists had attacked when he was there? What if one of my loved ones is where the next attack happens? What if the attacks start happening outside the big cities of the world? What if?

As I write, my phone dings with another text from Kim, the wife of our son Josh. She has been sending photos from Brazil where Josh is meeting her extended family for the first time. They're having a grand adventure, and it's wonderful to see them happy. But hanging out in the back of my mind are news reports about Zika and athletes who are dropping out of the upcoming Olympics in Rio de Janeiro for fear of contracting the virus. Before they left, Josh assured me they'd be wearing long sleeves and bug repellent. The photos I've received of the suntanned couple in tanks and T-shirts reveal that he's already forgotten his first promise. I'm left with a can of Off! to comfort me.

And I already told you about yesterday.

Again, it is a peaceful morning. And again, there's no guarantee my day will proceed as it has begun. The sober reality of my life is that I am not in control. The ensuing sense of vulnerability behind that truth is enough to overwhelm a soul with anxiety.

Fear Not . . . Why Not?

"Fear not" is a popular refrain in Scripture. But why *not* be fearful? This is a frightening time to live! The ills of our world are real. Are we supposed to merely deceive ourselves with delusional platitudes of divine safety?

I love the hymn "A Mighty Fortress Is Our God." It reminds us of God's greatness and might. But the real reason I love it is because it acknowledges the very real power of Satan. I know that sounds strange, but stick with me.

> For still our ancient foe doth seek to work us woe.
> His craft and power are great and, armed with cruel
>   hate,
> On earth is not his equal.
> Did we in our own strength confide, our striving would
>   be losing.

> Were not the right man on our side, the man of God's own choosing.
>
> Martin Luther

There's something empowering about acknowledging and confronting the truth about our fear. Kind of like peeking under the bed or creaking open the closet to check for monsters. Reality is scary, but our imaginations are often worse. Facing our fear allows us to determine whether it is imaginary or real and to respond accordingly. As humans, the reality is that we are no match for our enemy: "on earth is not his equal." If it's only about our strength pitted against Satan's, we'd better get our sorry selves home real quick and go into lockdown. "Did we in our own strength confide, our striving would be losing." If we were alone, we'd be right to be in a constant state of anxiety. So how do we respond to the temptation to be anxious?

> The Lord is at hand; do not be anxious about anything, but in everything by prayer and supplication with thanksgiving let your requests be made known to God. (Phil. 4:5–6)

In most translations of this well-known passage in Philippians, verse 6 begins with a new sentence: "Do not be anxious." But the English Standard Version backs up a bit to the previous verse and begins the sentence, "The Lord is at hand; do not be anxious." (Remember, the chapter and verse divisions of Scripture were added as a tool. It's important to look backward and forward.)

That phrase, "the Lord is at hand," makes all the difference. It brings to mind a small, frightened child in a thunderstorm. "You're okay, honey. Daddy's here." Because her strong and loving daddy is with her, everything is going to be okay. She is comforted because her trust is rooted in her father's presence and love, not by her understanding of her circumstances. The thunder and lightning are still loud and fearsome. But everything is all right because her father is "at hand."

Whether our circumstance is a monster under the bed, thunderstorms that shake the house, or Satan himself, it's only half the reality. The rest of our reality is that *we are not alone*! Jesus is Emmanuel, God with us. His power and presence are our ultimate security. His love for us is sure and has been proven: "But God clearly shows and proves His own love for us, by the fact that while we were still sinners, Christ died for us" (Rom. 5:8 AMP).

As beloved children, we are comforted by our Father's presence and secure in our prayers and thankful supplications as we make our requests known to God. The result is his peace: "And the peace of God, which surpasses all understanding, will guard your hearts and your minds in Christ Jesus" (Phil. 4:7).

It's a peace that goes *beyond* our understanding and steadies and sustains our hearts in the worst circumstances. Look at this same verse in the Amplified Version:

> And God's peace [shall be yours, that tranquil state of a soul assured of its salvation through Christ, and so fearing nothing from God and being content with its earthly lot of whatever sort that is, that peace] which transcends all understanding shall garrison and mount guard over your hearts and minds in Christ Jesus. (AMP-CE)

That peace, *true* peace.

Close to Home

It was my worst fear. I couldn't imagine how I could ever handle having a child suffer, much less die. I was pregnant with our first child, and we were attending the funeral of the seven-year-old son of our dear friends. He had died due to complications with leukemia. The memory of standing in line to offer our condolences after the service is vividly etched in my mind. My royal blue dress with the gold buttons down the front was just beginning to stretch slightly across my growing belly. I stood there with one hand holding on to Jeff and the other guarding the small swell as anxiety began to build a mansion in my mind.

Jim and Debbie loved God. They'd prayed for their son's healing. Our whole church had prayed! But Ian died. Some had the callous audacity to suggest that his death was due to hidden sin or a lack of faith. But I knew better, which presented an even more challenging problem than such a foolish idea. God could have healed Ian, but he didn't. *Why?* It wasn't long after the birth of our son Joshua that the reality of God's control—and my lack of it—sank in. Anxiety completed construction and moved in.

I couldn't watch the news or any scary or sad movies. I was afraid to take Josh out of the house. I even questioned Jeff's ability to keep him safe. It was all up to me, and even though I doubted I was up to the task, I would kill myself trying. If I didn't, the anxiety would.

Josh was just a few months old when late one night I lay crying in bed, voicing to Jeff the anxiety that was consuming me.

"You have to release Josh to God and trust him," Jeff said gently but firmly.

"I can't," I argued. "If I do, God might decide to take him like he did Ian."

"God might decide to do that whether or not you release Josh. You're not in control; he is." Jeff called out my delusion. "If you don't trust him, you'll never have peace."

And so began my sober and endless journey to release the souls I love more than life and to learn to trust a God I can't see.

Two and a half years later, I found myself in a hospital with Josh's six-week-old little brother, Daniel. After weeks of inexplicable projectile vomiting and a day of dry diapers, I knew something wasn't right. The pediatrician confirmed my fears and sent us directly to the hospital for an ultrasound and probable surgery to repair pyloric stenosis, a malfunction of the muscle between the stomach and small intestine that causes vomiting and dehydration.

The ultrasound confirmed the pediatrician's diagnosis. It was a minor surgery, but it would require Daniel to go under general anesthesia. According to the doctor, that was the greater risk. This was the very scenario I had dreaded, and I was certain it would undo me.

Daniel was admitted and put on IV fluids to rehydrate him before the surgery the next morning. Throughout the whirlwind of activity, I was just waiting to lose it. I knew it was coming any moment and just hoped it wouldn't be as ugly and embarrassing as I imagined.

When Jeff gets here, I'll collapse. But I didn't.

When he leaves and I'm alone with Daniel, I'm going to fall apart. But Jeff left, and I stayed together.

When they take him for the surgery.

When he gets back.

When I see the incision.

And so on.

My breakdown never came. Instead, I heard the lyrics to the Scripture memory songs I'd been listening to the last few weeks playing in the back of my head. Words of hope, promise, and peace made their way to my conscious thought every time I needed them. It was amazing! That evening, I held and sang to Daniel late into the night with the knowledge that these could be my last hours with him.

That might sound melodramatic. I don't really know how at risk Daniel was. I only know that the young mother *I was* shouldn't have been so calm. Something had changed in me that gave me the security to face my present and possible impending reality with a peace I'd never known before. A peace "which surpasses all understanding." *That* peace.

Daniel survived his surgery, and we went home the next day. Twenty-four years later, Daniel bears a small scar on his stomach. I have a scar too. It's on my heart along with dozens more, reminders of God's ability to sustain me through the unthinkable and turn my greatest fears into places of deep intimacy and trust in his power and goodness.

Anxiety's Grip

Anxiety is a powerful motivator—powerful enough to fuel a lifetime of striving. As women who seem to be programmed to love, nurture, and care for our families and friends, we are uniquely susceptible to anxiety and fear. Care that causes concern can transform into worry in a millisecond. For some of us, that slippery slope is the only path our hearts know. But the rotten fruit of fear is destruction.

The alternative to anxiety and fear is trust, but trust seems so amorphous. It sounds good, but how do we catch and hold on to it? It's like a bubble—a pretty idea that doesn't seem to hold up in the face of our trials, real and imagined. So we turn to fear as if it were something more solid and tangible. But fear doesn't change anything. Not only is fear destructive, it's also futile: "And which of you by being anxious can add a single hour to his span of life? If then you are not able to do as small a thing as that, why are you anxious about the rest?" (Luke 12:25–26).

Obviously, we need something concrete to hold on to when we're afraid. For the rest of this chapter, I want to look more deeply at three common responses to fear and anxiety. As we consider these familiar responses, it's my hope that you will discover not only the wisdom, joy, and freedom of trusting God but its *pragmatism* as well.

I had a nightmare last night. It was the kind that wakes you up with your heart beating out of your chest and then draws you back in because it feels more like reality than your crumpled sheets and warm pillow. It tosses you back and forth a bit before it surrenders and leaves you lying wide-eyed, staring at the ceiling, heart pounding, and talking yourself down from the cliff edge of anxiety.

We've all had that kind of dream. It leaves us somewhere between "that was absolutely ridiculous!" and "what if something like that really happened?" or "why in the world did I dream *that*?" Thankfully, dreams in the dark don't make much sense when analyzed in the morning light. As frightening as nightmares can be, the anxiety they induce is usually smoothed away as we make the bed, putting our minds and sheets back in order.

The anxiety that robs us in our waking hours is of a more subtle variety. It comes in the back door, squatter like, and looks for its opportunity to blend in unnoticed. It has many disguises: busyness, harsh words, control, manipulation, anger, yelling, and sarcasm, to name just a few. And we typically respond to it in one of three ways: denial, delusion, or despair.

Denial Is Not Just a River in Egypt

I'd prefer not to acknowledge my mind's "squatters." Maybe if I pretend they're not there, they'll go away. But while unwarranted fear is destructive, the very real threats of life demand a response. Ignoring them is dangerous. Consider this scenario: you're lying in bed. It's 2:00 a.m., and you awaken to hear banging outside your window, then whispering—maybe even words that suggest dastardly plans. As much as you might wish your sweet sleep had continued uninterrupted, you'd be foolish to turn up the fan, roll over, and snuggle back in. On the other hand, you might freeze in fear. But if you're smart, you'll pull out your inner superhero, grab your phone, and call 911. The anxiety of an impending threat is your call to action.

But that's an extreme example. Take something more common like an overdue bill, a big one. Now there's some anxiety! When your budget is already stretched between one grocery trip and the next with barely enough room for your favorite coffee indulgence once a week, there are all kinds of temptations to ignore the Mt. Kilimanjaro bill at the bottom of the stack. "Maybe next month," you tell yourself again, ignoring the impending threat of further fees and financial consequences. Does that hit too close to home? It does for me. Been there. I'm not suggesting the solution to something like this is simple. I don't have a money tree or a wealthy grandparent. But I do know that responding to the anxiety with denial only digs me deeper into difficult circumstances. Whether it's a nagging relationship issue, a bad habit, finding a lump on my body, or a big bill, responding in denial to the anxiety these things induce is dangerous.

Possibly the *most* destructive aspect of denial is the means to which we go to keep ourselves floating on the deceptively smooth waters of *de Nile*. I'm talking about those "Nah, nah, nah," fingers-in-the-ears manipulations of our minds and emotions, also known as our escapes: food, television, shopping, sleep, social media, or just one more glass of wine. They're the good gifts of God that we misuse in our desperation, things that might be fine in their proper place but are potentially destructive and futile as a response to anxiety and fear.

You Can Call Me Captain

"I've got this."

The delusion of control is heady and hard won. We chase it down with new planners and articles and books or with the latest system, online course, gizmo, or gadget. Education, vocation, nutrition, recreation: they're all tools we pull into our arsenal to protect ourselves from life's inevitable anxieties. Tools have their place. They're useful. But when they quit being anything but a *servant*, beware!

As I learned to release my children to God with each birth, including two preemie babies who collectively spent a month in the NICU, I loosened my grip a tiny bit. But even though I knew their lives and deaths were beyond my control, I was determined to make whatever lives they did have as safe and secure as possible. Of course I was! I was their mom. Keeping them safe is part of the job description, right? Yes. And no. (We'll talk more about this in chap. 8.)

Survival is good, and safety is an effective means toward that end. But hanging out at the starting gate of parenting, as well as any other endeavor we care deeply about, are those squatters. We may begin with pure motives and our eyes focused on the finish line, but the more we care about a thing, the more anxiety will be there to trip us up.

Want to feed your family nutritious food? Awesome! But between the endless and often conflicting information and limited resources of time and money, trying to feed your family nutritiously can produce an ulcer.

Concerned about your child's education? Of course you are! But the options are many, and culture seems to be convinced that your child's entire future and well-being hinge on which option you choose for preschool. After you've agonized and finally made your choice, you discover it was only the first of hundreds of choices you will have to make over the next twelve-plus years of your child's academic life.

And the list goes on. Forever.

The theme song for my mothering became an anything *but* harmonious, two-part dirge playing on repeat in my head. The lyrics alternated between "I'll never be enough" and "I'm going to get my act together." I bought fully into the delusion that if I tried hard enough, went fast enough, got up early enough, prayed and read my Bible enough, and did a soul-sucking amount of every-last-thing-I-could-think-of enough, I would *finally* get my act together and somehow *be* enough. Control. It was how I faced down those parenting anxieties.

Routine and order have never been my strength. I'm great at making plans and buying planners but struggle to execute said plans. I could give you plenty of explanations from all the personality tests I've taken over the years as to why this is not a strength of mine, but whether you are a natural Martha Stewart of efficiency or not, the relentless and delusional pursuit of control will eat your lunch every time. And if it can't take your lunch, it will be content with your stomach lining.

Like the obsessed Captain Ahab, we hunt the great white whale of control with a mixture of fear and vengeance. The delusion is deceptive. Moby Dick is bigger and stronger than any boat, and he has an agenda too: ruin. We chase the delusion of control at the cost of our souls.

Drowning in Despair

I did it again. I checked Facebook right before bed. Another attack, tearful sympathies expressed for France, a new hashtag. And desperate posts.

"When will this end?"

"This has to stop!"

"Lord, have mercy. Please."

Undeniable. Absolutely beyond any delusions of control. Despair.

It seems to be crouching at the door of all our hearts recently. While many women have lived with such violence throughout the world and history, it's somewhat new to our relatively safe and comfortable, Western, twenty-first-century lives. Until 9/11, most of our acquaintances with terrorist attacks came via the news. But after that day, when almost three thousand lives were lost, over six thousand injured, and millions changed forever, "safe" became tenuous. Now it seems we are imploding as our culture turns on itself, and violence from both within and without our borders escalates.

When our anxieties and fears have given birth to a reality that won't be denied or controlled by the most Herculean of deluded efforts, despair makes sense. It is logical—that is, if we are by ourselves and on our own.

> On that day, when evening had come, he said to them, "Let us go across to the other side." And leaving the crowd, they took him with them in the boat, just as he was. And other boats were with him. And a great windstorm arose, and the waves were breaking into the boat, so that the boat was already filling. But he was in the stern, asleep on the cushion. And they woke him and said to him, "Teacher, do you not care that we are perishing?" And he awoke and rebuked the wind and said to the sea, "Peace! Be still!" And the wind ceased, and there was a great calm. He said to them, "Why are you so afraid? Have you still no faith?" And they were filled with great fear and said to one another, "Who then is this, that even the wind and the sea obey him?" (Mark 4:35–41)

I was caught on the water in a storm once. Jeff, eighteen-month-old Josh, and I had spent a few days at his parents' house on the river. It was our last day there, and we were ready to head home. We went down to the dock to check on the boat before we left. It had rained the night before, and the bilge pump hadn't done its job. The floor of the boat was covered in a couple inches of water. Jeff said we needed to take it out, get it up to speed, and pull the plug out so the water would drain. That sounded suspiciously counterintuitive to me, but Jeff was the expert. I suited Josh up in his little Ninja Turtle life vest, and we headed out. The rain was still coming down but not too hard. As we gained speed Jeff pulled the plug, and the water began to drain. His plan was working, until we ran over a crab pot that wrapped itself around the propeller blade and brought us to a full stop. Jeff struggled to get the plug back in, as all the water we'd managed to lose and then some rushed back into our boat.

The rain and wind were picking up. Thanks to the crab pot, our motor was useless, and the waves were pushing us toward the rocky shore. Jeff said we'd both have to get *out* of the boat and push it away from the rocks. Remember, Josh was with us and was remaining *in* the boat while we literally jumped ship (now there's some therapy)!

We successfully evaded the rocks, and wide-eyed Josh was still sitting in the boat when we climbed back in. Jeff began furiously rowing with the one oar in the boat—until it broke in half.

Now the rain was pouring down. The waves were rough and high and getting rougher and higher. Our motor and solitary oar were broken. We were headed toward the rocky shore again. And Jesus was *not* taking a nap in the back of our boat.

Our desperate circumstances were undeniable. They were beyond any delusions of control. Despair seemed fitting.

Then we saw a boat headed our way from the shore. We waved wildly just in case they had some reason to be out on the water in a storm other than our rescue. As the boat headed our way, despair began to give way to hope. Our rescuer arrived and towed us back to shore safe and sound. The boat would need a few repairs, but the three of us walked away unscathed and with a great story.

Unlike our little family, Jesus's disciples were in the boat with *God in the flesh*—Emmanuel, God with us, the One who *made* the storm. Nevertheless, they gave way to despair: "'Teacher, do you not care that we are perishing?' And he awoke and rebuked the wind and said to the sea, 'Peace! Be still!' And the wind ceased, and there was a great calm."

What seemed to concern Jesus much more than their desperate circumstances was the lack of faith demonstrated by his disciples. He asked them, "Why are you so afraid? Have you still no faith?"

Their loving Lord was *at hand*. They had no need to despair.

The Strong Anchor of Trust

The flash of blue catches my eye and pulls me away from my anxious thoughts. The small indigo bunting looks like it fell into a vat of the deepest blue dye. It is brilliant. I watch it intently, soaking up its beauty as quickly as I can. I know it will fly away any moment. Tears quietly surface in my eyes. That's what beauty does. It reminds us of perfection. Eden. Home.

My soul resonates with the unblemished moment of perfect creation in the indigo bunting. Or a moment of music. A work of art. A scent. A sunset. They all evoke the perfection and intimacy we are homesick for—a glimpse and reminder of our Creator, a promise of our reunion.

It's no wonder anxiety eats away at our souls and our stomach linings. It's the opposite of what we were created for. It's an invader that taunts and threatens all that is holy in us and in our world, a threat that will rob us of the present, of our peace, and of our purpose. God knows how dangerous anxiety is, and he's taught us how to combat it. We must grant it no quarter.

> And though this world, with devils filled, should
>   threaten to undo us,
> We will not fear, for God hath willed his truth to tri-
>   umph through us.
> The Prince of Darkness grim, we tremble not for him;
> His rage we can endure, for lo, his doom is sure;
> One little word shall fell him.
>   Martin Luther, "A Mighty Fortress Is Our God"

If we were on our own, it would make sense to be anxious. "Were not the right man on our side," it would be reasonable to give in to the anxieties and fears that tell us to believe naive platitudes that "everything will be fine," to give our lifeblood to contrived efforts to secure our safety, or to stay home and pull the covers up over our heads.

Denial, delusion, and despair. So far our options don't look too great. They force us into a place of rational decision and help us to see that by not choosing to trust God in all our circumstances, we are at the mercy of our enemy.

Yet trust can seem so naive, and worry seems almost responsible. To onlookers, trusting God can look foolish, even *negligent*. And maybe it is a negligence of sorts—a turning away from the denial, delusion, and despair of a soul adrift with no anchor and turning toward the Savior who knows your situation better than you ever could and has promised to rescue you. Ralph Waldo Emerson recognized the peaceful fruit of this sort of negligence: "He will calmly front the morrow in the negligency of that trust which carries God with it, and so hath already the whole future in the bottom of the heart."[1]

There's a high cost to not trusting God. Daniel and I were talking the other day. After surviving his car crash, collapsed lung, and hospital stay, he is home safe, but with no car.

"How am I going to get to work?" Daniel asked. "I don't have the money to buy another car." I could hear the stress in his voice.

"Daniel, you need to trust God. You *must* trust God. This situation is bigger than you. I know you don't have the financial means, but if you don't trust God both you and your family will suffer under your stress. Making the choice to take each step and walk through this in faith is not an option. It's necessary!"

Ironically, it's almost easier to trust God when our lung is collapsed and we're lying by the side of the road or when our infant son is facing emergency surgery. When life spirals out of our control, we trust him because we are left without options. These desperate crises can become some of our most intimate times with God. We cry out, and he answers.

After we brought our newborn son Joe home from his three-week stay in the NICU, I prayed a prayer that I've prayed many times ever since: "God, you were so close to me in the hospital when I was facing the very real threat of the death of our son. You revealed your love, power, and presence to me in such personal and unmistakable ways. Can you please teach me how to trust you like I did when there was absolutely nothing I could do to change my desperate circumstances? I want to be that close to you every day and not only when my life is in crisis!"

God has been faithful to answer that prayer. He continues to teach me how to walk near to him, acknowledging *who* is on my side and trusting in his wisdom and power. Peace inevitably follows.

Jeff and I have been married thirty years. I trusted him the day I said "I do," but that trust is nothing like the trust I have in him today. Thirty years of living and loving have confirmed Jeff's trustworthiness. I trust him because I am well acquainted with him. Not only is he handsome and fun-loving, but he is also a strong and loving man of deep integrity. Throughout our many years of marriage, his love for me has been tried and found to be steadfast. I trust Jeff because I *know* him.

In order to trust God the way we must in a world full of anxiety, it's imperative that we become *well acquainted* with him and his attributes, character, and promises. Then we must make that acquaintance and knowledge our primary place of refuge—our go-to in both our crises and our everyday trials. He has given us his Word, and it assures us of his presence, protection, and peace. Even in the worst of storms.

QUESTIONS FOR REFLECTION

What are the top three sources of anxiety in your life right now?

How does knowing your Father is *at hand* comfort you?

After Paul reassures us of God's presence, he says, "Do not be anxious about anything, but in everything by prayer and supplication with thanksgiving let your requests be made known to God" (Phil. 4:6–7). Do you respond to anxiety by turning to God in prayer?

Why do you think Paul tells us to ask (supplication) with thanksgiving?

Have you ever experienced a peace that you couldn't explain? Describe it.

In what areas of your life is it hardest for you to trust God? Easiest?

What is your typical response to anxiety: denial, delusion, despair, or trust? Explain.

What moves you? How do these glimpses of God's perfection make you long for Eden?

Are you well acquainted with God? Do you know him well enough to trust him? How might you become more familiar with him?

His Sovereignty, My Security

*I will reject false security and embrace
God's sovereignty and provision.*

There is not a square inch in the whole domain of our human
existence over which Christ, who is Sovereign over all, does not
cry, "Mine!"

Abraham Kuyper[1]

A favorite game in our home is Snake Oil. The object is to create a product based on the card options in your hand and then sell it to the buyer who has also drawn a card telling them what character they are. On your turn, you are the salesman and your product is the snake oil. The most cunning salesmen start their pitch by telling the buyer why they *need* the seller's particular brand of snake oil. Having established a deficit in the buyer's gullible mind, the oily salesman explains why his product, and *only* his product, will meet that need. The buyer listens to all the pitches and chooses the most convincing product or *snake oil*. The irony.

In the end, if you get suckered into a bogus product, there's no loss—it's a game. But believing the snake oil salesmen of our day comes at a much higher cost. A woman can literally spend a lifetime on countless plans and potions that make fleeting and empty promises in a futile quest for security. How much time, energy, money, and dreams are wasted on modern-day snake oil?

As followers of Christ who "are not of the world" (John 17:14), we know that embracing God's sovereignty and his many promises of provision is the only sure way to be secure in this temporary life. Our Father's sovereign care far surpasses any security we could ever attain on our own.

Our Need for Security

Insecurity isn't an emotion we readily admit. But we know that life is fragile and that the threats against our happiness are innumerable. It's only natural and necessary to seek some semblance of security in our crazy world. The question is, Where will we look for it?

Finish this sentence in your head: "If only _____, I would feel secure." Whatever you put in that blank—*if only I owned a house in a nicer neighborhood*, *if only I were married*, *if only*—is where the enemy, aka the snake-oil salesman and father of lies, will try to seal the deal. I know! I have loads of half-empty bottles of snake oil in my mental medicine cabinet. Their labels read:

Get Your Act Together
Make Your Husband More Spiritual AND Romantic
Raise (Almost) Perfect Kids
Enlarge Your House, Your Bank Account, and Your Social Media Influence
Shrink Your Waist, Tummy, and Thighs
FINALLY Get the Approval You've Been Seeking

Sound familiar? I know. It's hard to admit to being scammed. We purchased these promises with excitement and swallowed them with a hopeful heart, but they turned sour with disappointment after just a few doses. And all the while, the enemy delights in his deceit.

Succumbing to these delusions isn't harmless. With every purchase, we buy into all kinds of self-reliant endeavors to preserve and/or transform ourselves into *our* ideals, according to *our* agendas, and on *our* timetables. Before long, God's grace is conspicuously absent. When we seek to find our security outside of God, we are in a vulnerable and dangerous place.

False Security

Throughout his letters to the early church, the apostle Paul consistently urged believers to "stand firm"[2] in the truth and freedom of the gospel. He knew it would take deliberate mindfulness to reject the world's solutions to the problems of life and to embrace truth. It was a necessary warning. The good news of the gospel was still hot off the press when the deceiver went to work challenging God's promises, just like he had way back in the Garden of Eden.

In Colossians 2, Paul warns believers not to be deceived and thereby *cheated* of faith's reward.

> Beware lest anyone cheat you through philosophy and empty deceit, according to the tradition of men, according to the basic principles of the world, and not according to Christ. For in Him dwells all the fullness of the Godhead bodily; and you are complete in Him, who is the head of all principality and power. (vv. 8–10 NKJV)

The believers at Colosse had succumbed to a

> Greek-influenced form of Jewish philosophy that viewed Christians as still vulnerable to spiritual forces. It was thought that these forces needed to be placated through veneration, through some sort of asceticism of food and drink, and by honoring certain days prescribed in Old Testament ceremonial law. . . . In Colosse, the Sabbath was kept and festivals observed in order to placate supernatural powers or angels thought to direct the course of the stars, regulate the calendar, and determine human destiny. This, Paul says, is a form of bondage from which Christ came to liberate men and women.[3]

Our ancestors were connected to the stars, calendar, and seasons in ways we take for granted. While we live our lives somewhat insulated with electric lights and air-conditioning, they were keenly aware of their dependence on the rising of the sun and the changing seasons for their livelihood. Their dependence gave way to superstitious beliefs. By necessity, "the tradition of men, according to the basic principles of the world," involved whatever means possible to try to control things that were essentially outside of their physical control.

Humankind's traditions have changed over the years, but the Colossians' deceit is not as far from ours as we might think. We may scoff at such primitive ideas, but the powers modern women seek to placate are just as demanding and insatiable. In the absence of dependence on the stars and seasons with which to threaten us, our enemy uses other created things. These modern snake-oil concoctions shift with the trends, but they tend to have one of a few things in common: a sense of necessity and legitimate control, pleasure, and/or distraction from our troubles—all things we look to for security. In a DIY world full of images of control, perfection, and beauty, there are plenty of opportunities for deception.

As insulated as our lives might be, we can't escape our sense of vulnerability to life's harsh realities. And even when we do manage to silence our *big* fears, we still stress. We stress over the disorganization of our closets and dresser drawers, the meals we served that looked nothing like the plated delights on magazine covers, our postbaby bodies that are softer than the hard bodies we so admire. Big or small, life-altering or trivial, these are all comparable to the traditions of men, which Paul warned the Colossians about. They are created things that promise security and demand obeisance and conformity.

Consider how our striving to placate these gifts rather than receive and enjoy them is similar to our ancient ancestors' temptations to appease the things they saw as necessary for security.

The sun, moon, and stars are gifts given to be enjoyed and to determine our changing tides and seasons. Likewise, modern created things are gifts to be enjoyed and tools to be used, but they're not our security. What's more, they're useless when it comes to eternal matters.

> Therefore, if you died with Christ from the basic principles of the world, why, as though living in the world, do you subject yourselves to regulations—"Do not touch, do not taste, do not handle," which all concern things which perish with the using—according to the commandments and doctrines of men? These things indeed have an appearance of wisdom in self-imposed religion, false humility, and neglect of the body, but are of no value against the indulgence of the flesh. (Col. 2:20–23 NKJV)

Look at that last phrase, "but are of no value against the indulgence of the flesh." All of the contrivances of the Colossians—don't touch, don't taste, don't handle—were efforts to fight their flesh, secure their lives, and ultimately perfect themselves. But Paul insists they are useless against fighting sin, "the indulgence of the flesh."

We sense deep within us that we are not enough. Why else would we strive so hard to *become* enough? As Christians, we are susceptible to the temptation to somehow perfect ourselves through seemingly good efforts. Paul exposes that idea for the lie it is. He knows that Satan is a subtle thief intent on stealing the true security of our salvation, which was bought at the ultimate price.

This seems to be one of Paul's greatest battles in the early church, and it continues to be ours today. We are forever buying into the slimy sales pitch. It begins with doubt (*Did God actually say?*), leads to lies (*You will not surely die . . . you will be like God*), and ends in striving, separation from God's love and provision, and ultimately destruction. True security is found only by trusting in God's sovereignty and provision.

The Difficulty of Sovereignty

The sovereignty of God is a difficult concept, to say the least: an omniscient, omnipresent, omnipotent God who works *all* things according to his divine will.[4] Immediately, the loaded questions begin waving wildly like hungry reporters at a press conference.

"But, Mr. God, if you are truly all you say you are—all-knowing, all-present, and all-powerful—why don't you intervene to stop the evil of our day?"

"Excuse me, Mr. God, in case you haven't noticed, our world is going to hell in a handbasket. If you're sovereign, why don't you do something?"

These aren't new questions. God's enemies have hurled them like spears in an effort to deconstruct rational belief in a sovereign God, even as followers of God have wrestled with them throughout history, a struggle well documented in Scripture. While these seemingly conflicting realities present a difficult challenge to our limited minds, we can take comfort that we're in good company.

I'm not going to attempt to give a comprehensive defense of the doctrine of God's sovereignty here. First, I'm not qualified. There are learned men and women who have devoted themselves to this apologetic, and I recommend you search them out. Second, that kind of explanation is beyond the scope of this book.[5]

Lest you think I'm copping out, here is where I *do* stand: the Bible affirms God's sovereignty over and over again both explicitly and in its stories. If God's sovereignty is on trial, I'm a character witness (along with Moses, Daniel, Job, Peter, Paul, and others). I know him to be trustworthy, powerful, and proven by both my personal experience and the experiences of millions throughout history. As we briefly touch on the doctrine of God's sovereignty in this chapter, I'm going to ask you to embrace it *as a matter of fact* supported by Scripture and faith. Ultimately, I don't know any other way to approach it. We simply can't fully comprehend it, and I believe the humble stance of trust is our best bet at gaining some understanding of this glorious and powerful truth.

There's another reason embracing God's sovereignty is difficult. It requires the relinquishment of control, or at least the illusion thereof. Despite all the evidence that we're not in control of our lives—a snake-oil bestseller—we long to believe it. But demanding our own agendas keeps us striving to conform our lives to *our* ideals. Like playing the children's picture games in which we'd try to identify what didn't fit, we look at our lives with an eye focused on "what's wrong with this picture?" The zebra doesn't fit in the barnyard. The couch doesn't go in the kitchen. The puppy doesn't belong in the basket of kittens. This _____ (fill in with your present trial) doesn't belong in my life. We become hyper-focused on whatever is currently "wrong" with our life's picture and, in the meantime, fail to see the grace God is sending us daily through his Word, creation, and the body of Christ.

Entrusting ourselves wholeheartedly to a sovereign God we can't even see, much less comprehend, is a lifelong process. It's hard, but it's our surest hope for security. The first step is surrender.

Surrendering My Agenda

Most of us can look back at situations in our lives that seemed to have no purpose for good. But in hindsight, we can see how

God used difficult and even destructive trials to bring about his good purposes in our lives.

> For my thoughts are not your thoughts,
> neither are your ways my ways, declares the LORD.
> For as the heavens are higher than the earth,
> so are my ways higher than your ways
> and my thoughts than your thoughts. (Isa. 55:8)

"As the heavens are higher than the earth." That's how much higher our Father's ways and thoughts are than ours! Is it any wonder we so often don't understand him?

The relationship of parent and child has gone the furthest in helping me to understand God's sovereign hand on my life and to surrender my agenda.

Do you remember when you were thirteen, and you had it all figured out? Your parents just didn't understand! Or even better, have you been the parent of a thirteen-year-old who had it all figured out? You likely know the frustration of both parties. But as a parent or adult interacting with teens, you see the limitations of their experience and knowledge. They believe they see the whole picture, but you know they see only part of it. It's all they can see. In order to believe you, they have to trust you.

When our youngest son, Sam, was three years old, we lived in a house that backed up to the woods. Lyme disease was prevalent in our area, so I was constantly checking the kids for ticks. One day I found one on Sam's tummy. I carefully pulled it off, but the head stayed attached. I was unable to remove it, so we went to the doctor.

It was the classic traumatic pediatric experience. Two nurses and I held Sam down, while the doctor attempted to remove the tiny tick part. It probably took all of two minutes, but in mama-time, it was an hour.

Sam screamed, "It hurts, Mama! It hurts, Mama! It hurts, Mama!" over and over again. His cries broke my heart. Still, I held him firm. I saw the whole picture.

Finally, the doctor was successful. I gathered the sobbing Sam into my arms, and we were left alone in the exam room. I sat rocking and comforting Sam, who continued to whimper: "It hurt, Mama. It hurt, Mama. It hurt, Mama." The tears stopped, but the pitiful mantra continued all the way through checkout and to the parking lot.

Sitting in the car, he continued, "It hurt, Mama. It hurt, Mama. It hurt, Mama." And I could hear the confusion and unspoken questions in his voice.

"Why did you let them do that, Mama?"

"Why didn't you stop them, Mama?"

"Why did you *help* them hurt me, Mama?"

"Didn't you know it hurt, Mama?"

What struck me was how Sam was seeking my comfort even in his confusion. Throughout his physical trial, he'd cried out for help to no avail; now he continued to express his sadness, all the while accepting my comfort. Eventually, he settled down, and we made our way home.

Short of singing my praises, Sam behaved like a psalmist that day. He cried out for help. He asked, "Why?" And he sought comfort in the arms of his parent. *He trusted me even when he didn't understand.* Like our Father, I had a perspective on the situation that Sam couldn't have. I understood and felt compassion for his cries and knew they were only partially informed. All Sam knew was that it hurt, and that's what motivated him to cry out and then to complain. I didn't hold that against him; instead, I comforted him. While he didn't understand, I did.

It's a simple story, but Sam is a picture of us. His three-year-old knowledge of his situation was actually much closer to mine as an adult than my knowledge is to an infinite God's. Again, is it any wonder we so often don't understand him? Our surrender and trust cannot be based totally on understanding. God is gracious and has revealed much about himself and his ways: his creation tells of his wonder, we have his very words, and he's given us his Son and the glorious truth of the gospel. Nevertheless, he is beyond our understanding,[6] even intentionally.[7]

It's a strange dichotomy. Crying out in desperation for relief and trusting the One to whom I'm complaining enough to let him comfort me in my trial. *My* agenda is relief, and right now, please. If relief was God's agenda, he would change circumstances and lift pain immediately from our lives, even before we cried. In fact, why wouldn't he prevent it altogether? We know he can—he's sovereign. Clearly, he has something else in mind: "For those whom he foreknew he also predestined to be conformed to the image of his Son" (Rom. 8:29).

The world offers many promises of security, but it's a security that is false—false because there is no real security in the preservation of our unsanctified flesh. God's agenda for our lives is to conform us to the image of Christ, to make us like Jesus. This life isn't about me simply becoming my personal best and avoiding trouble and pain. The reality is, if we are followers of Jesus, our lives are no longer our own: "You are not your own, for you were bought with a price. So glorify God in your body" (1 Cor. 6:19–20). Can we sit here a minute? This is quotable Scripture, the kind you may have memorized in Sunday school. Like many familiar things, its significance can sometimes get lost.

We love our independence here in the West. A whole culture has been built upon it! But when Paul spoke these words to the Corinthians, they understood the concept of a person being owned. Slavery was real, just as it has been throughout history in most places in the world, yet it's fairly foreign to us. Granted, it has a negative connotation. Isn't the message of the gospel freedom?

Yes. We have been freed *from* the slave master of sin. But we are not autonomous.

> Do you not know that your body is a temple of the Holy Spirit who is within you, whom you have [received as a gift] from God, and that you are not your own [property]? You were bought with a price [you were actually purchased with the precious blood of Jesus and made His own]. So then, honor and glorify God with your body. (1 Cor. 6:19–20 AMP)

The word translated as "your own" is *heautou*.[8] It literally means "yourselves." Paul is telling us *you are not yourselves.*

> For he who was called in the Lord as a bondservant is a freedman of the Lord. Likewise he who was free when called is a bondservant of Christ. You were bought with a price; do not become bondservants of men. (1 Cor. 7:22–23)

> And they sang a new song, saying,

> "Worthy are you to take the scroll
>   and to open its seals,
> for you were slain, and by your blood you ransomed
>   people for God
>   from every tribe and language and people and
>   nation,
> and you have made them a kingdom and priests to our
>   God,
>   and they shall reign on the earth." (Rev. 5:9–10)

These verses confirm the truth that we've been purchased with the blood of Jesus. You've likely heard that phrase a hundred times. Initially, it may have struck you as gory. But then you came to understand the reality of Jesus's sacrifice on the cross and how it bought your salvation. His blood, like the sacrifices of old, covered your sin and made you clean before a righteous and just God.

Yes, we are free. But we will be ruled by something. If it's ourselves, then we are taking the place of God. Bottom line, we are not *ourselves*. We find true freedom when we surrender our agendas and our lives to the One who has secured our freedom.

> I appeal to you therefore, brothers, by the mercies of God, to present your bodies as a living sacrifice, holy and acceptable to God, which is your spiritual worship. Do not be conformed to this world, but be transformed by the renewal of your mind, that by testing you may discern what is the will of God, what is good and acceptable and perfect. (Rom. 12:1–2)

Embracing God's agenda to conform us to the image of Jesus allows us to see trials in a new light.

> Count it all joy, my brothers, when you meet trials of various kinds, for you know that the testing of your faith produces steadfastness. And let steadfastness have its full effect, that you may be perfect and complete, lacking in nothing. (James 1:2–4)

We are logical people. We don't like pain, and we do what we can to avoid it. Without an understanding and a realignment of our hearts and heads, rejoicing in trials just doesn't make sense. But when we recognize that trials perfect our faith, which produces steadfastness, which perfects *us*, it makes sense to rejoice. Through our trials, we are becoming more like Christ!

God has given us the wonderful promise that he is accomplishing his purpose and our good through our trials: "And we know that for those who love God all things work together for good, for those who are called according to his purpose" (Rom. 8:28). When we understand that the *good* God is working is part of his eternal purpose, we can wholeheartedly say (like Joseph said to his brothers[9]), what was meant for evil in our lives, God meant for good.

The transformation from a death grip on our agendas to the security of God's sovereignty involves change. When our security is based on protecting and preserving our lives, we will live in insecurity. But like every good parent, our heavenly Father is most interested in what is truly best for us. He will use trials to train our hearts to trust him, because he knows that the center of his love and sovereign will, whether it brings trials or blessings or both, is the most secure place we can be.

Remembering that his agenda is to conform us to the image of Christ helps us to submit our wills and trust in his goodness and wisdom when we can't understand his ways. The next two verses in Romans 8 reveal the Father heart of our God:

> For those whom he foreknew he also predestined to be conformed to the image of his Son, in order that he might be the firstborn among many brothers. And those whom he predestined he also called, and those whom he called he also justified, and those whom he justified he also glorified. (vv. 29–30)

God's power and sovereignty are not capricious. Rather, they are two of the most telling truths regarding his nature. He uses them to bring us into his family as he conforms us to Jesus "in order that he might be the firstborn among many brothers." He knew us, predestined us, and called us so that he might justify us and one day glorify us. We can trust him.

In order not to be conformed to this world, I must surrender my agenda of pleasure and comfort and embrace his agenda of conforming me to the image of his Son. The irony is that when I surrender my agenda, relinquish my rights to myself, and present my body as a sacrifice that is still alive and available to do whatever God calls me to, I not only find freedom, but I also find security. It's a security that could never be obtained by anything I could do. It is sure, because its source is the eternal, sovereign God.

The Security of Sovereignty

We would all like to be assured of a smooth, prosperous life free of relational conflicts, illness, financial struggles, and heartbreak. But this mindset reflects the "tradition of men" that tells us a (relatively) trouble-free life is necessary for security. But that is false security. God tells us he is all that is necessary.

While embracing God's promises of provision may be an easier task than embracing the mystery of his sovereignty, if we fail to acknowledge and trust in his sovereignty, we will miss his provision. And seeking security outside of God's provision is ultimately the protection and preservation of what I have or can obtain on my own. It doesn't involve the trials and struggles that are necessary for my sanctification.

When we reject false securities and embrace God's sovereignty, we receive the incredible assurance that the One who is I AM[10] has promised to care for us. The security we find in the truth of God's sovereignty allows us to live our lives with courage instead of denial, delusion, or despair. It's like facing the monsters in the closet and under the bed and finding out they really are there. We *know* we're not immune to pain, sorrow, and the multitude of things that threaten our well-being. It's a scary reality to confront, but when we face life and all of its sober realities with faith and trust, we realize there's provision for it. There's hope! It's hard and sobering but solid and comforting.

We've faced trials, and there will be more. The whole earth groans, waiting for its redemption, and we groan right along with it.[11] But because of the truth of our good God's sovereignty, we have a sure hope for the future and security and provision to navigate the present.

This truth has become fundamental in my relationship with God. The more I choose to take refuge in him and his promises of grace and strength when hard times come, regardless of whether or not they make sense to me, the more I find peace and security in his love.

> "The LORD is my portion," says my soul,
> "therefore, I will hope in him." (Lam. 3:24)

QUESTIONS FOR REFLECTION

Where, besides God's sovereignty, are you tempted to find your security?

What "created things" have you put your hope in?

How have you strived to *become* enough on your own?

Is it difficult for you to trust in God's sovereignty? If so, how? If not, why?

How difficult is it for you to surrender your agenda?

Do you believe that you don't belong to yourself but to God? Is that comforting or challenging or both? Explain.

Have you embraced God's agenda to conform you to the image of his Son?

PART 3

The Gospel's Price

A Dialogue with God

Meet me here
where heart beats with hope
and life looks bright

I'll meet you here
where hope prevails
even in darkness of night

Meet me here
where I pat my own back
for all I've accomplished

I'll meet you here
where my arms surround
though your day was fruitless

Meet me here
in the midst of my plans
for good times and laughter

I'll meet you here
where plans dissolve into tears
and my peace flows after

Meet me here
where loved ones surround
and make life feel secure

I'll meet you here
where heart aches lonely
but my presence is sure

Meet me here
where I'm strong in mind,
spirit, and speech

I'll meet you here
where weakness mutes words
and my strength is increased

Meet me here
where joy is abundant
and life is worth living

I'll meet you here
where despair overwhelms
and you meet me in thanksgiving

Meet me here
wherever life takes me
for you I'll be waiting

I'll meet you there

Ideal or Idol?

I will reject idols posing as ideals and embrace sacrifice, suffering, and hope.

You shall have no other gods before me.

God (Exod. 20:3)

The Old Testament stories of Rachel, Laban's daughter and Jacob's second wife, and the Israelites' golden calf are fairly familiar to most Christians. But like many Bible stories their familiarity can become a roadblock between the stories and the lessons they're meant to impart. When we take time to examine them more closely, their relevance to our modern lives can be surprising!

Rachel had already had a rough time of it. Her father had swapped her out for her sister on her wedding night. Then after some wheeling and dealing, she'd been made part of another deal—Jacob could have her also, but he would have to agree to work for seven additional years. She and her sister took sibling rivalry to a new level with a twisted "baby race," which she lost by a mile. Now her family was running away from her deceitful father, who had continued to exploit his son-in-law. They would flee while Laban was busy fleecing his flocks, a task at which he excelled equally with sheep *and* people. A lifetime and all she had ever known would be left behind as she followed her husband to a foreign land. With little time to pack, Rachel had to decide what to leave and, even more importantly, what to take. She grabbed her father's idols.[1]

The Israelites were tired. For centuries, theirs was a life of slavery, and now home was a nomadic life in the desert. Wandering and waiting, they'd followed their leader, who'd followed their God. But now, forty days since Moses had left them to meet with God, it seemed they'd both gone AWOL. Without the security of their leader, they looked for another. A shiny gold one would do.[2]

A Matter of Trust

Idolatry is a foreign concept to most of us in the twenty-first-century West. The idea of bowing to a statue seems archaic. In light of Scripture, idolatry seems especially ignorant. We read the numerous accounts of God's people returning to idol worship and shake our heads in wonder. How were the people of God so easily deceived? How could they have been so foolish? Even God called them "stiff-necked" (Exod. 32:9). After all he had done for them, after all his miraculous power they had witnessed firsthand, how could they have rejected God and turned back to idols?

But our indictment of them may be our own as well. As odd as idol worship seems to us, it was simply a matter of trust. Would they trust the God who delivered them again and again, forgave them again and again, and gave them his sure promises? Or would they turn their hearts and trust to the idols of their day?

Our modern-day dilemma is no different. Let's take a second look at these two examples. As we consider the circumstances and the people's responses, we may find more similarities than we first imagined.

Rachel had grown up in a pagan household ignorant of the one true God. She'd been taught by example to trust in her father's household idols. When times were bad, she'd watched him bow and petition these small gods. The lesson was that *this is where we go when we're in need.*

So when she found herself on the brink of a scary new life, Rachel grabbed for what she knew: "Laban had gone to shear his sheep, and Rachel stole her father's household gods" (Gen. 31:19). It was logical. It was a matter of trust.

The Israelites had scraped and scrapped under the oppressive heel of the Egyptians for centuries. It seemed their God had gone radio silent to their cries for deliverance—until Moses. Their rescue was dramatic and complete, as God plagued and plundered the Egyptians on their behalf and sent the Israelites out of Egypt with the wealth of their former masters.[3] Fast-forward. Their leader has disappeared, and they consider what resources they have. Suddenly, God's provision becomes more than mere gold and silver—it is the makings of another god. The influence of Egypt and their former pagan surroundings surfaces, groupthink takes over, and they turn from the one true God to an idol made with their own hands and from their own resources: "They have made for themselves a golden calf and have worshiped it and sacrificed to it" (Exod. 32:8). It was a matter of trust.

Worshiping and petitioning idols were common and accepted practices in ancient times, and it still is in many parts of our world. Their idols were simply what they chose to put their trust in. In times of need, it made sense to turn to them. They'd learned this through family and cultural practices. Idolatry was quite natural.

Modern Idols

Dear friends of ours have spent their entire adult lives as missionaries in foreign places where idolatry is openly practiced. Years ago, they were in the states with their family and visited us. It was fascinating to talk with them and hear their perspective as Americans who, being removed from the culture, had a more objective point of view. I'll always remember how surprised I was when they expressed that the idolatry of our country was worse than where they worked to share the gospel: "The idols of the West are disguised and hidden. People don't recognize their idols for what they really are."

They went on to explain how our idols aren't typically found in temples or candlelit shrines. Rather, they're parked in our garages, hanging in our closets, and growing in our bank accounts. They're hiding in our computer screens, credit cards, refrigerators, and often even in our relationships. They are masters of disguise, and they're what we turn to in trust. While more subtle and deceitful than its Old Testament and foreign counterparts, idolatry is alive and well in our modern material and relational idols. Like Rachel and the Israelites, we turn to the idols in which our culture has taught us to trust.

Quite often, our idols pose as *ideals*. They come in every shape and size. Ideals are what sell our books and determine our culture's trends. They promise health, knowledge, beauty, esteem, security, confidence, happiness, and more.

Ideals can be useful. They define our lives and the paths we choose. They're deeply personal, and they reflect the image of God's unique design for each of us. Surrendered to him and kept in their proper role and function of service, they are a gift and can serve us effectively.

But in our concerted efforts to achieve these ideals, they can slowly morph into idols.

And idols don't serve. They enslave. When we turn to our ideals in fear and make desperate grasps at self-sufficiency, we make the mistake of the Israelites. The resources given by God become our own "golden calf." And we bow.

My own experience with idolatry follows that pattern. I saw a *good* thing. Marriage, family, service in the church—all things that were gifts from God and could be a blessing to me and a means of sharing God's love and truth with others. But the means became an end as I struggled to "do it right." My ideals subtly morphed into idols as they became the standard for my self-worth, security, happiness, and peace. My weaknesses weren't areas in which to deepen trust in God and to experience his grace and strength. No. They were liabilities, and my idols had no tolerance for them. Day after day, I fell short of their unrealistic and incessant demands to be better, try harder, and work faster. My golden calf was ravenous and insatiable.

Grace, forgiveness, gospel—they were words that I could sing about, define, and point you to in the Scriptures. But in my self-determined pursuit of righteousness, I became a Pharisee and was pitifully guilty of their same error:

> This people honors me with their lips,
>   but their heart is far from me;
> in vain do they worship me,
>   teaching as doctrines the commandments of men.
>   God (Matt. 15:8–9)

Idols can be hard to detect in our day-to-day lives. An idol isn't necessarily something that is inherently sinful. It can even be a good thing, as it was for me. What makes something an idol is its subversive preeminence over God. Our wandering hearts have a way of taking God-given desires, gifts, and ideals and turning them into virtuous-looking idols.

This description of an idol is one way to determine where idols might be hiding out in your heart: *an idol is anything that I choose over God and his will as revealed in Scripture or anything I will sin for.* If I will choose to sin for a thing, there's a good chance that thing has become an idol in my life. Ouch. Another effective litmus test to unmask the idols in our lives is simply to ask ourselves, "When I'm being squeezed by life's trials, what do I turn to?"

Idolatry isn't looking quite so foreign anymore, is it?

A Jealous God

Do you remember the Bible story about the day the Philistines stole God? I bet you never thought of it that way. But when they captured the ark of the covenant in 1 Samuel 5, they stole the representation, if not the literal presence, of God. In his love and mercy for his people, God had made a way to forgive their sins and restore relationship with them. And it all took place at the *mercy seat*.

> And you shall put the mercy seat on the top of the ark, and in the ark you shall put the testimony that I shall give you. There I will meet with you, and from above the mercy seat, from between the two cherubim that are on the ark of the testimony, I will speak with you about all that I will give you in commandment for the people of Israel. (Exod. 25:21–22)

When the Philistines brought their trophy home, they placed their enemy's "vanquished" God in front of their "victorious" god, Dagon, as was customary. The next morning, Dagon was found lying prostrate in front of the ark of the covenant.

> Then the Philistines took the ark of God and brought it into the house of Dagon and set it up beside Dagon. And when the people of Ashdod rose early the next day, behold, Dagon had fallen face downward on the ground before the ark of the LORD. (1 Sam. 5:2–3)

They set their god upright, only to find him flat on his face again the next morning. And this time his head and hands were broken off. (In an ancient custom, the victorious would remove the head and hands of their dead enemies.) God wasn't messing around. And just to make sure the Philistines understood who they were dealing with, God plagued them with tumors. Wherever the ark went, the plague of tumors followed.

God's righteous war against idols extends from Eden to our day. He is a jealous God and refuses to share what is rightfully his—the fidelity of his people. As a married woman, I get this. My husband is a great guy! He's handsome and friendly. *And he's all mine.* Sure, you can be his acquaintance or friend. But when it comes to the love and affection that's meant for a wife, he doesn't share that! Nor do I share the affection due my husband. Ever. The very nature of our relationship is *exclusive.* In this covenant of marriage, there will be no other women besides me, and there will be no other men besides him. There's a lesson here for us.

God's demand for our wholehearted fidelity is reflected in our understanding of marital fidelity. It's quite natural. If my husband's attention and affections were to begin to turn toward another woman, *all* the alarms would signal and the red flags would be at full mast. Even the thought of it unsettles me. *This* is what is going on when our hearts turn toward and trust in other "gods" in our lives. Our merciful Father and righteous God has made it clear: "You shall have no other gods before me" (Exod. 20:3). Idolatry is infidelity.

If the idol Dagon fell before the representation of God in the ark, the idols in our lives will certainly bow before our God. God had no tolerance for the presumptuousness of the Philistines, and they were his enemies. How much more will he not tolerate idolatry in his own beloved children? In his righteousness, justice, and mercy, he will have no other gods before him. When our world feels like it's crashing down around us, it might just be God wrecking our idols.

Fear to Faith

The Israelites were witnesses to God's deliverance and power over and over again, yet they still turned away from God. We have witnessed them too. Nowhere is this more evident than in the message of the gospel. The mercy seat on top of the ark of the covenant was testimony to the merciful heart of God and his desire to be in relationship with his people. His mercy and love were so great, he would extend them even at the highest cost—the life of his Son: "For God so loved the world, that he gave his only Son, that whoever believes in him should not perish but have eternal life" (John 3:16).

We have witnessed his power through the resurrection of Jesus, and we have received deliverance through this great gift of salvation. So how is it that we are still tempted to turn in trust to lesser "gods"? Why are the following words of the cherished hymn "Come, Thou Fount of Every Blessing" so painfully true?

> Let Thy goodness, like a fetter, bind my wandering
>   heart to Thee.
> Prone to wander, Lord, I feel it, prone to leave the God
>   I love;
> Here's my heart, O take and seal it, seal it for Thy
>   courts above.
>
> Robert Robinson

Why are we so "prone to wander" and leave the God we love? At root, fear might be the greatest threat to our fidelity to God. Fear motivated both Rachel and the Israelites. In the face of uncertainty, they grasped at control, a fruit of fear. What could they grab hold of that would bring some sense of security? Some sense of certainty in their chaos? Some sense of peace, even if it was temporary and might get them in big trouble? They just needed *something* to take the edge off their immediate fear.

Family practices had taught them what to run to. Their surrounding culture had made their idolatry acceptable, even encouraging it. And in the case of the Israelites, groupthink was hard at work as well. These are the same influences that train *our* hearts and minds and teach us, for good or bad, where to place our trust. If we're not on guard, fear leads us to delusional and frantic efforts to control. Our fear of suffering and pain can drive us straight into the arms of idols, where we are promised the hope of relief even as those idols wrap us in their chains of slavery. Ultimately, we turn to idols in a desperate attempt to escape our trials.

On the other hand, God doesn't promise freedom from suffering. He promises freedom from sin. He *uses* suffering to make us more like Christ, and he offers new life and the hope of eternity in the midst of suffering. Jesus prayed, "I do not ask that you take them out of the world, but that you keep them from the evil one" (John 17:15).

But fear is a fact of life. God knows that. It's why he says over and over in Scripture, "Fear not." If you've been around the church most of your life like I have, you've probably heard something to the effect of "'Fear not' is a command." As a young believer, I heard that and felt like a failure or, worse, a sinner every time I felt afraid. I couldn't just *make* myself not be afraid. I didn't understand why God would command me to do something that seemed so impossible—until I found these verses in Psalm 56:

When I am afraid,
    I put my trust in you.
In God, whose word I praise,
    in God I trust; I shall not be afraid.
What can flesh do to me? (vv. 3–4)

"When I am afraid." The psalmist David was afraid! He even had a plan for what to do *when* he was going to be afraid. He would trust in God. I was off the hook.

Have you ever comforted a small child in their fear? "It's okay. I'm here. I'll take care of you. Don't be afraid." I imagine this is the heart of our gracious Father when he tells us not to be afraid—understanding, sympathetic, patient.

And then there's the kind of *fear not* that's more like a kick in the butt.

Have I not commanded you? Be strong and courageous. Do not be frightened, and do not be dismayed, for the LORD your God is with you wherever you go.
                      God (Josh. 1:9)

Like a good father, our heavenly Father knows when to hold and comfort us and when to drag us out from under the covers and push us out the door. Either way, he is with us, and we can trust him.

Our fear doesn't have to lead us away from God, to fearful efforts to control, and ultimately into the slavery of idols. *When* we are afraid, we can trust in God. Fear can be the catalyst that draws us to the safety of our Father's arms and to greater maturity and deeper trust, as we face our trials. Fear can lead us to faith, and faith is "the assurance of things hoped for, the conviction of things not seen" (Heb. 11:1). When fear leads us to faith, we experience God in a way that only happens when we walk with someone through a trial. We know this. When we walk through hard times with a family member or friend and come out on the other side, there's a bond of trust that doesn't develop any other way. The relationship is deepened, and we know where to go when we need someone we can trust. We've found a faithful friend. Fear that leads us to respond in *faith* to God ultimately leads us to fidelity—loyalty and commitment that have history, understand the sacredness of the bond, and won't be sacrificed for temporary and counterfeit peace.

Sacrifice

> Consider it nothing but joy, my brothers and sisters, when-ever you fall into various trials. Be assured that the testing of your faith [through experience] produces endurance [leading to spiritual maturity, and inner peace]. And let endurance have its perfect result and do a thorough work, so that you may be perfect and completely developed [in your faith], lacking in nothing. (James 1:2–4 AMP)

It's been said that God's kingdom is an upside-down one. Nowhere is that statement truer than in the Bible's teaching about trials and suffering. These are the upper-level courses in Christianity. You can be sure there's no Suffering 101. These classes are at least 300 level. They're where Christians graduate from milk to meat. And they aren't electives; they are required courses. God knows that we'd never choose them on our own.

James tells us that the endurance we need to become spiri-tually mature is the *fruit* of our trials and the *means* of our perfection in Christ. This is why we can and should "consider it nothing but joy" when we face trials. We're being made more like Christ.

This all sounds great while we're sitting here with our quiet and coffee. I'm writing, and you're reading. We nod our heads in agreement. Our spirits whisper a sincere *yes*. We want to be like Jesus, and it fills our hearts with hope to know the things that interrupt our days and wreck our life plans might not be the disasters we think they are. They might be the very things God is using to draw us closer to him and his will for our lives.

But what about when we're in the middle of the chaos, and everything in us is screaming, *No. No. No! How could* this *possibly be a part of God's plan?* Or when, like the Israelites, we wonder if he hears us in our distress. When our trials aren't theoretical but *terrible*, how do we "consider it nothing but joy"? Jesus shows us how:

> Therefore, since we are surrounded by so great a cloud of witnesses, let us also lay aside every weight, and sin which clings so closely, and let us run with endurance the race that is set before us, looking to Jesus, the founder and perfecter of our faith, who for the joy that was set before him endured the cross, despising the shame, and is seated at the right hand of the throne of God. (Heb. 12:1–2)

Kingdom living requires a long view on our circumstances. Jesus was willing to make the ultimate sacrifice because of "the joy that was set before him." His love for us and for his Father's will gave him the ability to endure the cross and all its shame. If, unlike Christ, we insist on remaining focused on our immediate circumstances, our world, and our kingdom, we will know only frustration and heartache. Trials and suffering will be consistent roadblocks to our goal of temporary and immediate happiness and security. But if by faith we take the eternal and long view—our perfection in Christ—we will be able to accept, and even embrace, our trials with joy because of the hope we have.

The book of Hebrews calls Jesus the "founder . . . of our faith." His incarnation, death, and resurrection are the "first cause" of our salvation. Some translations call him the *author* of our faith. He is also our faith's *perfecter*. And as James tells us, he uses trials and suffering to perfect us.

Like Jesus, we too are called to offer our lives as a sacrifice, an offering to God. Paul says this is our *reasonable* or *logical* response to our salvation.[4] Our obedience and willingness to sacrifice our lives to fulfill God's will in and through us emulate the response of Jesus to his Father. Jesus is our model. As we run the long race before us with endurance and by faith, he also shows us how to suffer.

Suffering

Suffering is a fact of life, but we try to avoid it as much as possible. Arguably, our suffering begins the day we are born into this cold world, where we hunger, feel pain, and cry. We cry from the moment of birth. Something deep within us knows this isn't how it is supposed to be. Even before we have words, we know that we are made for Eden, and this isn't it. Our harsh initiation is only a foretaste of the pain to come.

Probably the least claimed "promise" in Scripture is Jesus's assurance to us of suffering.

> I have told you these things, so that in Me you may have [perfect] peace. In the world you have tribulation and distress and suffering, but be courageous [be confident, be undaunted, be filled with joy]; I have overcome the world. [My conquest is accomplished, My victory abiding.] (John 16:33 AMP)

Even as I study and write these words, I'm discovering that suffering does not have a minor role in a Christian's life. It is inevitable. But for the follower of Christ, it is also purposeful and hopeful. Like the believer, suffering has been redeemed. We don't have to fear it. When we bravely face the reality of suffering in this life, we are able to see beyond the present pain to the good work and future glory that God promises to those who endure. More than merely resign, the Christian can in faith *embrace* suffering, because of the hope of glory.

Suffering takes on as many shapes as humans have thoughts. There is suffering so horribly indescribable, it is undeniable. And then there is personal suffering that, if compared, hardly seems deserving of the title at all. But suffering can't be objectively rated. It is deeply personal and therefore indefinable except by the sufferer.

When I awake each morning, though the fog of sleep has barely dissolved, I am already aware of my present trials and suffering. The news of the day may offer me perspective, as it makes me aware of the greater suffering of others, but it will not nullify my own suffering. Often, we try to talk ourselves out of our suffering by comparing it with that of others. We feel our troubles are unworthy of any acknowledgment and attention because so many have it much worse than we do. On the other hand, we can obsess over our suffering and trials, allowing them to consume our thoughts and emotions. Either response, denial or obsession, is ineffective and lacks faith.

But acknowledging our suffering without being overwhelmed by it is a task that is greater than us and our own resources. It's human nature to minimize or maximize our trials. Faith enables us to humbly accept our circumstances and our inability to rescue ourselves, but it doesn't leave us there. Faith moves us *through* the immediacy of our pain and *to* our hope in God and his love and power to bring about his good will in our lives.

But we have this treasure in jars of clay, to show that the sur-passing power belongs to God and not to us. We are afflicted in every way, but not crushed; perplexed, but not driven to despair; persecuted, but not forsaken; struck down, but not destroyed; always carrying in the body the death of Jesus, so that the life of Jesus may also be manifested in our bodies. (2 Cor. 4:7–10)

Acknowledging suffering is not complaining. If it were, the apostle Paul would be the biggest whiner around. In his many letters, Paul detailed his past and/or current suffering. But he *wasn't* complaining. Paul's purpose in communicating his pain was to highlight God's faithfulness.

As we consider our own suffering, both past and present, we can see God's faithfulness to us as well. Rather than ignore or be consumed by the pain we've known, we can allow our suffering to be a means of encouragement and strength to us and those around us.

Past Sorrows and Present Pain

A few years had gone by since I'd discovered Emily's struggle with cutting. The pain of it was in our past. Both Emily and I had learned much about God's grace, and freedom marked our lives and relationships in ways we'd never known before. Our present felt bright and full of hope.

And then one day I caught a glimpse of Emily's scarred stom-ach. It gutted me. While her scars were testimony to God's faithfulness and grace in our lives, they also testified to my failure as a mom. I'd let my daughter down. The sorrow was heavy; some days it still is.

When I watch my children fight their own battles with per-fectionism and self-worth, I see the enduring, rotten fruit of my own failures. It's painful. I've often asked God why he didn't teach me the lessons of grace while the kids were still little and before I'd harmed them. Maybe we could have avoided a lot of pain and regret. Even though I know he has worked out his will, was all of that really necessary? I know young moms who already have a beautiful grasp on God's grace, and it informs their mothering. Why couldn't that have been my story?

Like scars, the painful parts of our family's story are still a tender place—a place of humility, sometimes full of sorrow. Many days I've longed for a do-over. But this place of mixed memories has also become a place of deep trust and intimacy with God. I don't know why his time line is ordered like it is. But I do know his ways are perfect and much higher than mine.[5] Learning to trust God in this raw place has enabled me to pray with freedom. As I ask God to meet my children in their brokenness, I trust that their suffering will become a path to trust in God in their lives as well. It seems to be a prayer he is pleased to answer.

Some of our baggage has someone else's initials on it. The suffering and sorrow of our past is marked by the mistakes of others as well. This can be even harder to accept than our own failures. Injustices and unresolved relational pain work their way into our DNA. Our worldview is impacted by our experience and history, especially our childhood experiences. When we struggle to shake the ill effects of our past, our efforts can seem futile and maddening. Accepting God's good will even in the face of unjust suffering is impossible without faith. But we aren't alone. Scripture is full of God's sovereign will being worked out in the face of injustice. We can draw immense comfort from the many stories in Scripture of men and women who were treated unfairly and even abused, yet God worked their circumstances for their good. Like Joseph when he came face-to-face with the brothers who had sold him into slavery years earlier, we can say, "As for you, you meant evil against me, but God meant it for good" (Gen. 50:20).

The burdens of our past are not the only ones we bear. The suffering of living with present pain is a daily reality. Even Jesus acknowledged the pressing burdens of the day: "Therefore do not be anxious about tomorrow, for tomorrow will be anxious for itself. Sufficient for the day is its own trouble" (Matt. 6:34).

Suffering is as near as our relationships and our physical bodies. In fact, all our suffering has something to do with one or both of these. It is truly a reality of flesh-and-blood life. And there's no escaping it as long as we are still drawing breath.

> For we know that the whole creation has been groaning together in the pains of childbirth until now. And not only the creation, but we ourselves, who have the firstfruits of the Spirit, groan inwardly as we wait eagerly for adoption as sons, the redemption of our bodies. (Rom. 8:22–23)

Hope—the Good Fruit of Suffering

> For the moment all discipline seems painful rather than pleasant, but later it yields the peaceful fruit of righteousness to those who have been trained by it. (Heb. 12:11)

Our suffering is not in vain. Two of its many good fruits in this life are increased dependence on the Lord and relinquishment of our grip on control. Paul clearly expresses this in regard to his own suffering:

> For we do not want you to be unaware, brothers, of the affliction we experienced in Asia. For we were so utterly burdened beyond our strength that we despaired of life itself. Indeed, we felt that we had received the sentence of death. But that was to make us rely not on ourselves but on God who raises the dead.

He delivered us from such a deadly peril, and he will deliver us. On him we have set our hope that he will deliver us again. (2 Cor. 1:8–10)

Suffering also confronts us with the reality of our weakness and our practical need for God's grace and strength to navigate life's journey. Like Paul, we discover God's might and strength in our weakness: "For the sake of Christ, then, I am content with weaknesses, insults, hardships, persecutions, and calamities. For when I am weak, then I am strong" (2 Cor. 12:10).

Another fruit of suffering is the ability to truly empathize with the pain of others. There's nothing quite like offering truth that has been won in battle. That's where I've found a lot of peace as a mom. I want to comfort others who are also experiencing the inevitable trials of parenting. My battles were not in vain. They have purpose in the body of Christ as well as in my life. My scars are a license to honestly share my struggles and the lessons I've learned through them, to testify to God's faithfulness and love, and to give hope to others in the middle of their own suffering.

Blessed be the God and Father of our Lord Jesus Christ, the Father of mercies and God of all comfort, who comforts us in all our affliction, so that we may be able to comfort those who are in any affliction, with the comfort with which we ourselves are comforted by God. For as we share abundantly in Christ's sufferings, so through Christ we share abundantly in comfort too. If we are afflicted, it is for your comfort and salvation; and if we are comforted, it is for your comfort, which you experience when you patiently endure the same sufferings that we suffer. Our hope for you is unshaken, for we know that as you share in our sufferings, you will also share in our comfort. (2 Cor. 1:3–7)

Remember the story about Sam in chapter 5? His childlike trust in my love made it possible for him to receive my comfort in the middle of his pain. Our duty to comfort others has a prerequisite. We must experience God's comfort first. And in order to receive his comfort, we must trust him. Trust leads to our comfort, which leads to comfort for others, which ultimately results in a whole and healthy body of Christ.

There's no comfort quite like the comfort of "You too? Me too."

"You've felt crushed by your failures as a mom? Me too."

"You wrestle with anxiety in the morning? Me too."

"You get discouraged and want to quit life some days? Me too."

"You have seen God bring good out of pain and suffering? Maybe I will too."

"You keep pressing on and seeking God in faith? Then I can too."

It isn't that misery loves company but rather that humanity yearns for solidarity. Suffering is isolating, and we long to know we are not alone in it. As followers of Christ, we have the supreme comfort of Christ and those who have gone before us who've suffered immensely and found joy on the other side of pain.

> So we do not lose heart. Though our outer self is wasting away, our inner self is being renewed day by day. For this light momentary affliction is preparing for us an eternal weight of glory beyond all comparison, as we look not to the things that are seen but to the things that are unseen. For the things that are seen are transient, but the things that are unseen are eternal. (2 Cor. 4:16–18)

> Therefore, since we have been justified by faith, we have peace with God through our Lord Jesus Christ. Through him we have also obtained access by faith into this grace in which we stand, and we rejoice in hope of the glory of God. Not only that, but

we rejoice in our sufferings, knowing that suffering produces endurance, and endurance produces character, and character produces hope, and hope does not put us to shame, because God's love has been poured into our hearts through the Holy Spirit who has been given to us. (Rom. 5:1–5)

QUESTIONS FOR REFLECTION

Growing up, what did you learn to turn to when times were tough?

Which of your culture's idols are you most tempted by?

If idols are identified by what we trust in, what we turn to in hard times, and what we will sin for, what are the idols in your life?

Does knowing that idolatry equals infidelity help you to understand God's jealousy for his people? Explain.

Can you see a connection between the things you fear and what you are tempted to trust in and idolize?

Has there been a circumstance in your life that moved you from fear to faith? Explain.

How might a long view of your present trials inform your faith and help you to endure and even rejoice?

Do you tend to minimize your trials or be overwhelmed by them?

How does knowing that suffering is purposeful encourage you?

What are some of the good fruits of suffering that you've seen in your own life?

How have you been comforted by others who have suffered? How have you comforted others with the same comfort with which you've been comforted by God?

Liar, Liar, Pants on Fire

*I will reject dressed-up lies
and embrace naked truth.*

Lead me in your truth and teach me,
 for you are the God of my salvation;
 for you I wait all the day long.

Psalm 25:5

It was one of those times when you *know* you've heard God. Not audibly, but in your mind and heart in a way that—for all its inability to be explained, much less proven—is absolutely, undeniably real.

I was praying and in that familiar place of deep regret over the ways I'd failed as a mom. I could see the results in some of the things my kids struggled with now as teens and young adults. I knew God was meeting them in those hard places, and we'd seen so much love, forgiveness, and grace. But I couldn't help but wonder, *God, why didn't you teach me the things I understand now when the kids were small, before I hurt them?* It was the question that had nagged at me for years.

I could give you all the right answers to my question. I could quote the right verses, and I could smooth over my own sore scars and come to a tentative peace. But my question would still nag. I don't think I actually expected him to answer me.

I didn't tell you to write their stories. You're not the author of them. I am. *And you're not the hero of their stories.* I am. *But you're not the villain either. You're on my side, and you are a beautiful and powerful* part *of their stories.*

And a thousand pounds fell off my back. In that moment, God unmasked a lie I'd believed for far too many years, a lie that had burdened me unnecessarily and had robbed too much of the joy that was mine as a mother. It was a powerful, heavy lie, and its disguise was brilliant. But the naked truth my dressed-up lie hid was *glorious.*

Dressed-Up Lies

Dressed-up lies parade as truth. They're different from your average lie because they promise good things, virtuous-sounding things, even *godly* things. They're not the kind of lie that's told to cover up or tempt toward blatant sin. Instead, their deceit is found in their self-reliance. Dressed-up lies don't take faith; they put me in the driver's seat. The thing dressed-up lies have in common is a reliance on human effort. *If . . .*

> I read the right books, I'll have what I need to live my life the right way.
>
> I craft the best life, I'll be happy.
>
> I marry a good man, I'll be safe and loved.
>
> we get our kids involved in a good youth group, they'll be spiritually safe.
>
> we elect the right leaders, we will secure our children's future.

These decisions are important and worthy of careful thought. Empowered by the Spirit, our choices are powerfully influential in our lives. But alone, even the best-lived life isn't enough to guarantee the things we deem necessary and often the very things God has already promised to his children. So why are we so easily deceived by dressed-up lies? I believe there are at least two reasons: desire and ignorance.

We want to believe we can obtain the things necessary for our happiness and peace apart from a deep, daily reliance on God and his body, the church. Sin's seed in our hearts makes us rebellious and receptive to dressed-up lies that maximize self-reliance. *We want to be in control.* Our prideful desire for independence pushes us away from God, trust, and truth and toward the enemy and his lies. Satan knows we can't escape our neediness, so he stands by waiting to offer us dressed-up lies that deceive us and feed our self-reliance.

Ignorance of our design, how God has created us, also makes us vulnerable to dressed-up lies. We are made with a multitude of spiritual, relational, and physical needs: love, security, friendship, food, shelter, nurture, and much more. Dressed-up lies either promise counterfeits of these necessary things or lead to means of obtaining them that don't align with God's ways.

Lies usually fail to deliver, and when they do, the costs far surpass the benefits. But it's not enough to steel our wills and resolve to deny ourselves the things lies promise us. We need to look beyond the lies and investigate what it is that makes them a temptation. More often than not, we will find legitimate and good desires, things God has offered us, through his ways defined in his Word.

Naked Truth

Dressed-up lies sacrifice the naked truth because the truth seems too simple, too naive. Why would you trust in a God you can't see when you can take control and secure your own future? Why indeed! Unless you know the truth about the God you profess, trust is a foolhardy, illogical endeavor.

But what *is* truth? That's the million-dollar question, and the answer will define the direction of your life both now and forever.

> Then Pilate said to him, "So you are a king?" Jesus answered, "You say that I am a king. For this purpose I was born and for this purpose I have come into the world—to bear witness to the truth. Everyone who is of the truth listens to my voice." Pilate said to him, "What is truth?" (John 18:37–38)

What is truth? The answer can elude both the honest seeker and the hardened skeptic. In an article titled "The Truth Will Not Set You Free," the author writes, "We have long been taught that the truth will set us free, and that seeking the truth is a worthy goal. What if there is no absolute truth? What if there are just degrees of truth (or lies) that we tell ourselves?"[1] *What if?* This idea embodies the heart of Pilate's rhetorical question. If truth cannot be known, not only are we hopeless, but we're also sitting ducks for Satan's lies.

Fortunately, God does not leave this question unanswered. Here is just a small sample of Scripture's response to the question, "What is truth?"

> The sum of your word is truth,
>> and every one of your righteous rules endures forever. (Ps. 119:16)

Jesus said to him, "I am the way, and the truth, and the life. No one comes to the Father except through me." (John 14:6)

Sanctify them in the truth; your word is truth. (John 17:17)

This is he who came by water and blood—Jesus Christ; not by the water only but by the water and the blood. And the Spirit is the one who testifies, because the Spirit is the truth. (1 John 5:6)

It's no surprise that outside of a knowledge of God and faith in him, searching for truth is a dead-end pursuit. Nevertheless, the human soul is covered with the fingerprints of its maker. Separated by sin, it longs for reunion. That longing is articulated in the soul and, whether voiced or not, reveals itself in the question, "What is truth?" Eventually, every person ponders the meaning of life. The fact that we recognize that our lives require meaning is *itself* evidence of the existence of truth.

Ironically, any and every conclusion at which the pursuit of truth arrives is inherently *dependent* on truth. To say "there is no truth" is, in fact, a statement of either a truth or a falsehood. Falsehood itself requires the existence of truth.[2] This dilemma has the potential to bring a person to either salvation or destruction—to the reality of truth as a person or to denial. To deny truth is ultimately to deny Christ and to remain in bondage to sin. But, contrary to the previously mentioned article, the truth also has the potential to set us free.

> If you abide in my word, you are truly my disciples, and you
> will know the truth, and the truth will set you free.
>
> Jesus (John 8:31–32)

Truth Revealed

So why "naked" truth? Because I want to embrace truth *as it is*, not *as I'd like it to be*. As I'd like it to be: comfortable, no trials, no desperation, no tears, no pain—now or ever; the fruit of strong faith without the stretch. As it is: weeping for a season and joy that comes in the morning;[3] trials that produce endurance and the fruit of hope;[4] sacrifice and suffering that cut the apron strings of my heart to this world and tie them to eternity.

Embracing naked truth is a step of faith that we are called to continually as we walk life's path. Will I accept the many truths of God's Word and in faith allow them to be the filter through which I come to all the conclusions about my life, or will I embellish and "dress up" the lies I'd rather believe? Will I walk by faith or by my own limited sight?[5]

The wonderful thing about embracing God's truths, even when they stretch and test our faith, is that in embracing them we discover the reality and surety of his promises. A lifetime of turning our faces to his in faith results in a life enriched and sustained by the supernatural Creator of the universe. There isn't a lie that can be dressed up enough to even begin to compare with that!

I'm Not in Control

"God is in control." It's a statement of truth that can bring incredible security and freedom, but it can also make people angry. It can be perceived as flippant, an excuse, or passing the buck of personal responsibility. Sometimes, we simply don't want to give up the reins. For all our failures, there's still something satisfying about the delusion of control.

But the naked truth is that I am *not* in control. The longer I live, the more evident this truth becomes. My lack of control, however, doesn't excuse me from the responsibility of my decisions. It can be tricky to hold these two truths in tension. God is in control, and I am responsible for my actions. The principle of sowing and reaping reveals the harmony of what at first glance seems dissonant.

> Do not be deceived: God is not mocked, for whatever one sows, that will he also reap. For the one who sows to his own flesh will from the flesh reap corruption, but the one who sows to the Spirit will from the Spirit reap eternal life. (Gal. 6:7–8)

When my kids were young, this was a favorite verse of mine to share with them. I wanted them to understand there's no fooling God. One of my sons got tired of hearing this warning and suggested I "find a new verse." We laugh about it now, but the principle is fundamental and one that's easily and often ignored, to our own harm. Deceit is subtle and insistent, but at some point we will reap what we've sown.

This truth should both sober us and fill us with hope. It should sober us because the seeds I sow to my sinful flesh are powerful. Harsh words in a moment of anger live long beyond that moment. I may walk away and forget about it, but I have planted a seed that without repentance, forgiveness, and prayer has the potential to sprout and reap corruption.

But the truth of sowing and reaping is also full of hope. If I "sow to the Spirit," I will reap life. That means the seeds that I sow in faith will surely bring a harvest of righteousness.

There's another lesson in the verse that follows. Without its admonition, we are in danger of depending too much on our own efforts to "sow": "And let us not grow weary of doing good, for in due season we will reap, if we do not give up" (v. 9).

It's not a coincidence that Paul uses an agricultural analogy. Like the farmer who prepares the soil and sows the seeds, we have a responsibility to work diligently. But we must realize, all we can do is sow. *We have no power to bring forth life from a seed.*

My job is to sow seeds, and it's not an easy one. It involves clearing, tilling, planting, waiting, nurturing, and protecting until it's time to harvest. But without the miracle of the maker, all my effort is futile.

The miracle is the work of the Holy Spirit—the mystery. To forget this is to be vulnerable to all kinds of lies. What if I thought I had to make the seed sprout? What kind of needless and crazy efforts might I go through to make it happen, ultimately destroying the potential of the seed? Waiting for the promised harvest takes patience. If we do it without faith, we will become weary and resort to our own efforts. But if we don't give up, God promises we will reap the harvest of righteousness.[6] It's a promise and the truth.

I love Vincent van Gogh's art. The color, texture, and everyday-ness about his paintings inspire me to see my own everyday world with new vision. His painting *The Harvest* is one of my favorites, and a copy hangs in my living room. I distinctly remember a day some years back. I was lying on my couch, weary and discouraged from parenting teens. I'd sown until my whole body ached. What more could a soul do? But for all my efforts, my "fields" showed little sign of a harvest. As I stared numbly at Van Gogh's image of a valley ready for harvest, the truth of sowing and reaping slowly began to come alive, and I wrote this:

> You, Who gives seed to the sower, give me faith to scatter.
>
> I till the soil of young hearts—some still tender, others already rocky with the disillusionment of time and experience. The grit and gravel littered upon the ground by the enemy of this field.
>
> I wait for perfect weather. But the seasons fly fast, and this sower's seed lies waiting in my satchel. Can one plant in rain, wind, drought, and storm? The climate of this terra, this home, sees it all.
>
> Oh, to own the simple faith of the farmer. His efforts sown, he scatters knowing only One can make seeds grow. How foolish of me not to scatter seed, waiting for perfect conditions. How proud.
>
> I long for harvest and rejoice when seemingly fallow fields bear fruit.
>
> In the sowing, my dependence dies to self and arises to Another. Buried deep in the darkness of faith, life is called forth. Hope sprouts and reaches toward the light. From death to life.
>
> Resurrection is not my task.
>
> "Come sit with me, sweet child, dear son. Let me tell you of my Father."
>
> And all I do is scatter.

Blessings Are Gifts, Not Birthrights

> Some murmur when their sky is clear
> And wholly bright to view,
> If one small speck of dark appear
> In their great heaven of blue;
> And some with thankful love are filled
> If but one streak of light,
> One ray of God's good mercy, gild
> The darkness of their night.[7]

My plans for the future always tend toward the positive. Even as I sit with my planner each morning, I do not schedule what I know is inevitable. Every single day I will experience challenges, trials old and new, and some days even crises. But that reality doesn't get considered as I make my plans. How could it? I don't know what a day will bring, good or bad. Nevertheless, I plan for the good. I expect it.

If there's any single day in the year when I expect good things, it is December 25. Christmas mornings are pregnant with promise. As a child, I could rarely sleep the night before the most wonderful day of the year. Visions of all I'd hoped and wished for in the preceding weeks kept me awake counting the minutes and begging morning to hurry.

My wish list was a work of art. The Sears catalog was a dog-eared mess come mid-December. I would circle, highlight, and make detailed, prioritized lists so there would be no confusion for my parents as they chose my Christmas gifts.

At last, morning would arrive and with it all I'd dreamed. Family picture albums chronicle my and my younger sister's elated faces as we unwrapped and hugged our hearts' deepest desires and dreams come true—a tennis racket, a doll, a football, a hamster. Similar photos of *my* children fill my computer today. Their wish lists were made via the internet and emailed to us complete with links. The nature of their gifts, like their wish lists, tended to be much more electronic, but the elation on their faces was the same.

But I remember a Christmas that was unlike the other joy-filled mornings. There were gifts, some even from my list, but there was also disappointment. I didn't get all I'd hoped for. My visions had grown even larger than my hopes, and expectation stole my delight. My wishing had given way to entitlement.

As an adult, I've learned that as I make plans for Christmas Day, I need to recognize and make room in my plans for the inevitable. If I don't, my expectations can easily ruin the day with their demands of perfection. Christmas is a celebration of the greatest gift, and my plans need to reflect the humble and grateful heart of a recipient and beneficiary of the gift of grace. This is the state of mind that needs to frame *all* my days.

When I see the blessings of my life as gifts, not to be demanded or expected, I receive them in the true spirit of gratitude. Suddenly, I am overwhelmed by the flood of gifts in a day—breath, laughter, beauty, love.

Moses said, "I am not worthy of the least of all the mercies and of all the truth which You have shown Your servant" (Gen. 32:10 NKJV). His humble words perfectly reflect the proper posture of my heart. That I would receive so many gifts and so often in this dark, sin-cursed world is testimony to God's generosity. This perspective is a game changer!

We delight in receiving gifts. And as a parent, I delight in giving them. So does our heavenly Father.

> Ask, and it will be given to you; seek, and you will find; knock, and it will be opened to you. For everyone who asks receives, and the one who seeks finds, and to the one who knocks it will be opened. Or which one of you, if his son asks him for bread, will give him a stone? Or if he asks for a

fish, will give him a serpent? If you then, who are evil, know how to give good gifts to your children, how much more will your Father who is in heaven give good things to those who ask him! (Matt. 7:7–11)

This verse, like all biblical truths, is understood only in context. On its own, it may seem like Jesus is handing us a blank check and saying, "Ask for whatever you want." But its context is Jesus's Sermon on the Mount, also known as the Beatitudes, which have been called "the ethics of the Kingdom of God."[8] The *good things* he promises are the things that God says are good. "These gifts from the Father are the things Jesus has been describing as necessary for disciples: righteousness, sincerity, purity, humility, and wisdom. Those who know their own need will ask God for them."[9]

Following Christ requires a continual reformation of our concept of good. These good things *are* our birthright as "born-again" followers of Jesus. To comprehend and claim his promises, we have to align our heads and hearts with God's economy. When I begin to call good what he calls good, I will "seek first the kingdom of God" and therein find the good things necessary for both physical and spiritual life.[10]

My Identity Is Found Only in Christ

Dressed-up lies are attractive because they promise things that look deceptively like the things God promises. Naked truth reveals God's promises, which are not superficial. They're not something we put on, work hard to keep clean, and sustain by our own strength. The promises of God are the fruit of *who we are* in Christ—our identity.

At the moment of birth, we begin the quest for identity. Most of us are lovingly named by a mother and father. With this first declaration, identity begins its formation. Ideally, we are defined by the love that is shown to us as we grow. Our cries are responded to with compassion and comfort. We are told we are worthy of love as our parents nurture, protect, and guide us.

Flowing directly from the source of *their* identity come truths and lies that will continue to define us. *We are worthy when we behave. We are worthy when we get good grades. We are worthy when we excel.* Soon we begin to hear other voices. Culture is happy to chime in, and we begin to define our identity by what we choose to believe. All these voices can combine to bring us closer to Christ's love and truth or drive us further away. Most of us need to have our minds renewed when we closely examine the foundation on which we have built our identity.

Our source of identity is sometimes revealed by considering our highs and lows. What thrills me? What depresses me? What makes me do a happy dance? What makes me want to pull the covers up over my head and hide from life? What brings me the greatest joy? What makes me want to curse? The answers to these questions can reveal what I have built my identity on. Often, it's a good thing. For me, being a wife and mother was my pass-fail marks. When I was doing well by my judgment, I felt strong and secure in who I was. But when I was "failing," I felt fear, shame, and discouragement. I've also been tempted to build my identity on words—my own. One of the greatest joys of my life is speaking and writing to encourage women. I've had some success, but it can seem like it's never enough. That's another indicator of identity—it never quite comes through on its promises of ultimate fulfillment. That's because *nothing* is big enough to hold your identity as a creation of the eternal Creator. You have been designed to find yourself in Christ.

Once you begin to know and taste the security and peace of surrendering *the rightful authority to define you* back to your maker, surrender becomes easier because you experience the blessing of submission. Only God has the authority to tell you who you are.

I will speak more to this in chapter 9 when we focus on the beauty of your story. For now, recognize that the voice of your Father is full of compassion. His thoughts toward you outnumber the grains of sand on the seashore.[11] The promise is that finding your life in Christ[12] is finding your true self, your security, your greatest joy, and your Father's boundless love.

QUESTIONS FOR REFLECTION

What are some "dressed-up lies" you have been or are tempted to believe? What is the truth?

How has living in a relativistic culture influenced your view of truth?

How has Scripture influenced your understanding of truth?

How do you feel about the truth that you are not in control?

How have you seen the truth of sowing and reaping manifest in your life for good? For bad?

How do you feel about the truth that blessings are gifts, not birthrights?

Do you typically receive your blessings as gifts, or do you have expectations of good things that you believe you deserve?

How do you feel about the truth that your identity is found only in Christ?

Where else are you tempted to look to define your identity?

Women in Combat Boots

I will reject safety
and embrace the battle.

Pick up your cross. It's the only way you or anyone else can know a resurrection. Carry your cross so this carrying of pain makes love. It is never the cross you carry, but your resistance to the cross, that makes it a burden.

Ann Voskamp[1]

Emily's battle with an eating disorder wasn't quickly won. It's actually been a series of battles in what will likely be a lifelong war. Like most enemies, the temptation to believe the lies about food and God and self and life in general doesn't disappear. The enemy is always lurking. But Em has become a skilled warrior. She is alert to the enemy's strategies and knows how to defeat him in battle again and again.

Our mutual friend René is a retired lieutenant colonel with the US Air Force. Her twenty-two-year military career took her around the world and to eleven countries, some of which were battlegrounds. In each place she traveled, she wore combat boots. René retired, but she felt her boots' job wasn't yet done, and she gave them to Emily.

The boots definitely made a fashion statement, but Em, René, and I knew they said more than that. Emily wore them as a reminder to herself of the battle she was fighting. Day after day she laced up those big, clunky, black leather boots with the intention to fight. Safety wouldn't be found by denying the reality before her. It wasn't easy, but Emily chose to embrace the battle.

The Danger of a Safe Life

Most of my life has been spent with one goal in mind. More than happiness, more than material wealth, at times even more than love, I have worked toward safety. Safety is the preservation of *all* that I value. I may not be able to be sure of happiness, wealth, and/or love, but I can take measures to make myself safe. In fact, I can live my entire life avoiding danger and even risk, in order to secure safety. I can control safety. Right?

Safety is a high value. Our survival is dependent on it. We don't walk the street in the middle of the night, we lock our doors, we throw out spoiled food, we wear our seatbelts, and we teach our kids how to dial 911, all in the name of safety. It's almost a no-brainer. Of course we work hard at being safe. But when safety becomes the filter through which we make all our decisions, we not only eliminate risk but also eliminate opportunity and purpose.

Think about it. The most rewarding and purposeful parts of your life were most likely also the riskiest—sports, competitions, auditions, tests, college and job applications, marriage, childbirth. Almost everything we work hard for entails great risk. The risk and even the danger are what makes it rare, worthy, and of value.

I first shared this perspective on safety with moms. That was challenging. Moms are hardwired to protect their children, as they should be. To suggest that a mom could be *too* concerned about safety seemed almost counterintuitive. But our culture has made an idol of safety (as well as a lot of profit), especially when it comes to our kids.

Our son Ben was nineteen when he went to Uganda for ten days to work at an orphanage. The opportunity came about suddenly, and the funds did too. I'd always felt that it was important for our children to see other cultures and lifestyles, especially those of the body of Christ. But from the time he was young, I felt strongly that this was even more important for Ben. It seemed like this was the opportunity. Jeff and I prayed and believed Ben was supposed to go.

He would be traveling with his friend Grant, who hosted a Bible study Ben had been attending. I'd seen Grant but had never actually met him. Jeff had met him only briefly. Nevertheless, we said yes.

On the day of their departure, it hit me. *I've never met this guy, and my son is traveling to Uganda with him. Am I an idiot? How did we ever say yes to this? What were we thinking?*

That evening, I pulled up the airline website and watched Ben's plane as it flew over the Atlantic on its way to Turkey, then Rwanda, and finally Uganda. I had a decision to make. Would I trust that God had provided this opportunity and led our decision? Or would I give way to fears that made me doubt our decision because of the reality of risk?

Whether it's raising our children or living our own lives, if our supreme goal is safety, we won't take the risks God calls us to. There's a price to pay for not trusting God, and Jesus's parable of the talents illustrates it well. You can read the story in Matthew 25:14–30, but I'll paraphrase it for you here.

Jesus begins by saying that the kingdom of heaven will be like a man who was going on a journey. Before he left, he entrusted his property to three servants according to their abilities (this is where our word *talent* got its meaning[2]). Two of his servants invested their talents and multiplied them. But the third servant was afraid to risk, so he buried his talents in the ground where they'd be safe. Upon the master's return, his servants were called to give account of their stewardship. Of course, the master was pleased with the two servants who'd made a profit for him. But when the third servant revealed how "safe" he'd kept his talents, his master was furious. He called the servant wicked and lazy and condemned his inaction.

I'll admit, the first time I read this story, I felt more than a little empathy for the third servant. I *sympathized* with him! The poor guy was just trying not to lose what he'd been entrusted with. I would probably have done the same. Why was the master so harsh? Is that what God thinks of me when I play it safe? Lazy? *Wicked?*

But the master had a higher value than safety, and the servant's job was to steward what he'd been entrusted with *according to his master's values.* The risk of loss was a reality, but not to risk at all was the greater loss. Like the master, God values our faithful stewardship of the talents and opportunities he's given us even more than our temporary safety. He is eternal, as are we. The difference is, we easily forget that our life's purpose encompasses more than what we see in any given day. That's why Scripture is full of reminders:

> Do not lay up for yourselves treasures on earth, where moth and rust destroy and where thieves break in and steal, but lay up for yourselves treasures in heaven, where neither moth nor rust destroys and where thieves do not break in and steal. For where your treasure is, there your heart will be also.
>
> Jesus (Matt. 6:19–21)

> For what does it profit a man to gain the whole world and forfeit his soul?
>
> Jesus (Mark 8:36)

The apostle Paul embraced this mindset.

> For to me to live is Christ, and to die is gain. (Phil. 1:21)

> But I do not account my life of any value nor as precious to myself, if only I may finish my course and the ministry that I received from the Lord Jesus, to testify to the gospel of the grace of God. (Acts 20:24)

This mindset is compatible with risk. It is also compatible with the spiritual battle to which every follower of Jesus is called.

The Battle Is Real

I was born on a battlefield. I'm not unique; so were you. It sounds dangerous, but as followers of Jesus, we have been equipped with all we need to fight. What *is* dangerous is *forgetting* that we are in a battle.

So often we wake up, walk into our day, and walk onto the battlefield having forgotten we're in a war. Can you imagine what that would look like in an actual war zone of our day? It would mean sure and absolute defeat. When we forget that we have a real enemy whose very purpose is to "steal and kill and destroy" (John 10:10), we are sitting ducks for his attacks. But when we remember that our "adversary the devil prowls around like a roaring lion, seeking someone to devour," we will heed Peter's warning to "be sober-minded" and "watchful" (1 Pet. 5:8). We will also embrace the promises and truths of God in a way we might not have before. Recognizing the reality of our daily spiritual battles wakes us up to our need and to God's provision in a practical way and helps us to more fully appreciate the wonderful truth that, because of Jesus's death and resurrection, we've already won and are on the *offense*, not the defense.

> Finally, be strong in the Lord and in the strength of his might. Put on the whole armor of God, that you may be able to stand against the schemes of the devil. For we do not wrestle against flesh and blood, but against the rulers, against the authorities, against the cosmic powers over this present darkness, against the spiritual forces of evil in the heavenly places. Therefore take up the whole armor of God, that you may be able to withstand in the evil day, and having done all, to stand firm. (Eph. 6:10–13)

If you attended Sunday school when you were growing up, you are no doubt acquainted with this familiar passage. You may have even dressed up in the "armor of God" like my young boys did. Each piece of their plastic play armor was labeled appropriately, and of course, the "sword of the Spirit"[3] was the most coveted weapon. But Paul's charge is so much more than a Sunday school image. The figurative armor of God[4] is an absolute and literal necessity for every Christian: "For though we walk in the flesh, we are not waging war according to the flesh. For the weapons of our warfare are not of the flesh but have divine power to destroy strongholds" (2 Cor. 10:3–4).

There's often a disconnect between the reality of spiritual battle and our daily lives. It's easy to forget we're in a battle. Our forgetfulness may well be the most successful strategy of our enemy.

We read and agree with these verses that are meant to prepare us for our spiritual battles, but then we set them aside for only the *big* trials of our lives—the crises. And we set ourselves up to be pummeled by the daily battles we face. We can spend a lifetime wrestling "against flesh and blood," even our own, and never battle our true enemy.

But if we remember that we're in an unseen battle every day that is more real than what we *do* see, both our big and our small challenges and trials begin to make more sense. Our eyes are opened to the sin that has tripped us up. We see how Satan is resisting the work of God in our lives and the lives of those we love. We see division and conflict as more than personal; they're an attack on the unity of the body of Christ. We find a deeper motivation for life than our comfort and security. The Holy Spirit and his residence *in us* become the power we rely on. We embrace the battle and entrust our days and lives to God. And we join forces with Jesus in his incarnation and the eternal work it was meant to accomplish—freedom through the message of the gospel.

The Battle Is Ours

I've got good news and bad news. The bad news is that we don't get a choice in the matter. If we have chosen to follow Christ, we have enlisted in spiritual battle "against the rulers, against the authorities, against the cosmic powers over this present darkness, against the spiritual forces of evil in the heavenly places" (Eph. 6:12). The good news is that we were already in the battle before we made the choice to follow, but *now* we're on the winning side. We've won! Embracing the battle actually helps make sense of our lives and our trials. They are consistent with the battle we're in. Rather than seeing our pain and hardships as places of discouragement because things aren't working out the way we planned, we begin to see potential in them.

I often write in my sunroom in the early morning while it's still dark outside and the quiet inside helps me hear. This morning, as the light of dawn nears, it reveals a sky thick with heavy, ominous clouds. They threaten cold and rain. But in the east, a warm glow spreads low across the mountains. Shades of pink begin to appear and reflect across the underside of the clouds. The color grows higher and spreads wider until the sky looks like it's on fire, and the sun has yet to even crest the mountains. The menacing clouds have become the backdrop for the soon-to-arrive sun's glory. It is magnificent. So it is in battle. Our trials become the very thing that reveal God's strength and power in our lives.

For over two decades, I have struggled with autoimmune issues. They come and go, but when they come, they can derail my days with sickness and fatigue. They are the antithesis of what I think I need to be able to care for my loved ones and pursue the dreams God has given me. They are unwelcome at best and hated at worst. But my "flesh and blood" health issues aren't my enemy; they're just one of my battlegrounds. They're also the backdrop to God's glory as he reveals his strength in my weakness—the most important principle of spiritual warfare.[5]

One difficult morning, I was talking with Emily and asked her to pray for me. I felt terrible and as usual had too much to do to be feeling less than 100 percent or at least somewhere close. Em began to pray, and she asked God to "please give Mom strength to be weak." That was *not* what I had in mind when I asked her to pray. The only acceptable request was for strength. Period. I needed strength so I could be strong. *Strength to be weak?* It was an oxymoron!

But she was right. I needed God's strength to accept my weakness. I needed strength to trust him when I was feeling so much less than 100 percent. I needed strength to let go of my plans for my day and receive his. I needed *strength* to be *weak*.

Our battlegrounds are as varied as we are. They can change with the seasons and circumstances of our lives or remain the same for a lifetime. Whatever they are, our battlegrounds reveal the truth about who we are—finite, weak, vulnerable, and in need of someone more powerful than us. What we do when we are confronted with that revelation makes all the difference. Do we hold desperately to our delusion of strength, or do we humbly accept our need and his provision by faith? When we choose the latter, we are ready to be equipped with his armor.

One of the greatest and most destructive lies is that our battles are liabilities and therefore disqualify us from God's love and approval. How absurd! That would be like a general blaming a soldier for being under attack. Your battleground is not a courtroom trial. (Remember, you've already been to court and were found guilty but *not* condemned.)[6] When life's circumstances rally and rage against you, *you* are not on trial. Rather, your battleground is a *proving ground* for the power and sufficiency of God in your life and in specific circumstances. It's where God shows up and shows off, as he demonstrates his power on your behalf. You just need to be sure of two things: (1) who your enemy is and (2) that you've got your armor on.

The Battle Is On

Few of us have ever experienced the horror of battle. We may have read about it in the news or history books. We may even have a relative who has seen it firsthand. But for the most part, we have lived with the blessing of peace and security. As a result, the reality of spiritual battle and the figurative talk around it can be lost on us.

Our oldest son is in the military. When he decided to join, I remember questioning whether I, as his mother, should be supporting and facilitating his decision. Late one night, I was up alone and it hit me: our country is at war, and I'm helping my son become a soldier! Everything in me as a mom had always protected my firstborn son from danger. But as quick as I thought it, God spoke to my heart: *Before there was even one of them, all the days of Josh's life were written in my book. I created him with a purpose, and my plans won't be thwarted.*[7] At that moment, I knew that there is an appointed time and place for each one of us to die, and if that time and place for my son was on the battlefield, then nothing I did or didn't do would change that. It was a sobering realization, but it was also a freeing one.

With a son in the military, I feel more invested in the peace of our country than I did before. I have seen the sacrifice just a little bit more up close and know better now how the peace we enjoy comes at great cost to thousands who sacrifice to secure it. I also have a greater appreciation for the fact that a nation's peace is not a given. I hope that you and I and those we love will never know the reality of physical warfare. But if we do, I pray we'll have the courage to prepare and fight. We'd be fools not to.

Meanwhile, we can take what little understanding we have of physical battles and apply that to spiritual battles. God is not silent on this matter.

> Blessed be the LORD, my rock,
>> who trains my hands for war,
>> and my fingers for battle. (Ps. 144:1)

God's people have known both physical and spiritual battles throughout history. We have brothers and sisters in Christ today who are fighting both. The Old Testament is especially known for its epic stories of battles and displays of God's supernatural power. In his sovereignty, God sometimes even stacked the odds against his people so that his power and glory would shine.[8]

The story of King Jehoshaphat in 2 Chronicles 20 is a great example of God displaying his strength in weakness. A great multitude of the Israelites' enemies were marching against them. Jehoshaphat was afraid and cried out to God before his people. After declaring God's greatness and faithfulness, Jehoshaphat prayed, "O our God, will you not execute judgment on them? For we are powerless against this great horde that is coming against us. We do not know what to do, but our eyes are on you" (2 Chron. 20:12).

I wonder if King Jehoshaphat's people cringed a bit when they heard their "fearless" leader declare their imminent doom so blatantly and boldly? For those who trusted in the might of the Israelite army, I'm sure it was disheartening. Can you imagine hearing one of our political leaders take a mic and express something similar? "God, help us. There's no way we can defend ourselves against _____ (fill in the blank with our country's most threatening enemy). We have no idea what to do next. We're looking to you." While we might be glad to see our leader call on God, the reality of the power-lessness of our mighty military would probably shake us up. But for those Israelites who truly knew and trusted in their all-powerful, all-knowing, and all-present God, their ruler's desperate dependence on him must have been a tremendous comfort.

> Some trust in chariots and some in horses,
>> but we trust in the name of the LORD our God. (Ps.
>> 20:7)

There's nothing like an army marching against you to reveal where you've put your trust. Our trials do the same. Often, I find the spotlight of adversity reveals my own halfhearted faith. While disconcerting, King Jehoshaphat's ancient response offers both comfort and practical instruction to us today.

Jehoshaphat wasn't putting on a good face or simply spiritu-alizing the situation when he prayed before his people. Second Chronicles 20:3 tells us he was afraid and "set himself to seek the LORD" (NKJV). His response to fear was to seek help from God. It's that simple, but so often turning to God and his provi-sion is the *last* thing we do. Faced with circumstances beyond our control, it's tempting to fret, panic, or exhaust our own resources before we cry out to God for help. When we finally do pray, it can be halfhearted. But Jehoshaphat *set himself to seek the Lord*. The Amplified Version elaborates: "Jehoshaphat set himself [determinedly, as his vital need] to seek the LORD." The literal translation of the word *himself* is "face.'"So Jehoshaphat *set his face* with determination, knowing it was his vital need to seek the Lord. He was wholehearted.

Then he poses a series of rhetorical questions:

> O LORD, God of our fathers, are You not God in heaven, and do You not rule over all the kingdoms of the nations, and in Your hand is there not power and might, so that no one is able to withstand You? (2 Chron. 20:6 NKJV)

Questioning God during a crisis is common. What's different about Jehoshaphat's questions is the nature of his challenge. His questions aren't based on his own merit: "Haven't I served you faithfully? Haven't I rid the land of idols and sent out my priests to teach the Law of the Lord?" He isn't challenging God's judgment or his justice. Instead, he is recounting to God his own power, deeds, and faithfulness.[10]

Jehoshaphat reminds God, himself, and his people of exactly *who* it is they are depending on. In light of this, though their need remains desperate—they have no power—there is real hope of deliverance. They don't know what to do, but they fix their eyes on the One who *does* and is *able* to deliver them.

And he does! Not only does God defeat their enemies, but the Israelites don't even have to fight! The Holy Spirit comes on a man named Jahaziel, and through him God responds to Jehoshaphat's prayer:

> And he said, "Listen, all Judah and inhabitants of Jerusalem and King Jehoshaphat: Thus says the LORD to you, 'Do not be afraid and do not be dismayed at this great horde, for the battle is not yours but God's. Tomorrow go down against them. . . . You will not need to fight in this battle. Stand firm, hold your position, and see the salvation of the LORD on your behalf, O Judah and Jerusalem.' Do not be afraid and do not be dismayed. Tomorrow go out against them, and the LORD will be with you." (vv. 15–17)

The battle plan is simple—almost too simple:

Listen.

Don't be afraid because it's God's battle, not yours.

Go down against them. Just show up!

Stand firm in his strength.

Hold your position. In other words, don't turn and run.

And see the salvation, the might, the power, and the deliverance of the Lord on *your* behalf.

And they rose early in the morning and went out into the wilderness of Tekoa. And when they went out, Jehoshaphat stood and said, "Hear me, Judah and inhabitants of Jerusalem! Believe in the LORD your God, and you will be established; believe his prophets, and you will succeed." And when he had taken counsel with the people, he appointed those who were to sing to the LORD and praise him in holy attire, as they went before the army, and say,

"Give thanks to the LORD,
for his steadfast love endures forever."

And when they began to sing and praise, the LORD set an ambush against the men of Ammon, Moab, and Mount Seir, who had come against Judah, so that they were routed. (vv. 20–22)

King Jehoshaphat leads his people out the next morning with final instructions to believe in and praise and give thanks to God for his steadfast love. And his enemies are routed. In fact, they destroy each other!

For the men of Ammon and Moab rose against the inhabitants of Mount Seir, devoting them to destruction, and when they had made an end of the inhabitants of Seir, they all helped to destroy one another. (v. 23)

167

My Jehoshaphat

The premature birth of our son Joe at thirty-two weeks was my first "Jehoshaphat" experience. Joe was born with a blood infection and was gravely ill. He was our fifth child, so I was already an experienced mother. I knew how to feed, protect, and nurture an infant, but I had no idea how to care for one as sick as Joe. He was too tiny to nurse, and once he was stable, he had to be fed by a tube through his nose. The disease in his body was far beyond my ability to protect him. And the only nurturing I could do was to hold his frail, little, three-and-a-half-pound body against my chest and let him hear the familiar heartbeat of his mama. Utterly reliant on God and the knowledge and skill of the medical staff, I was "powerless against [the] great horde that [had come] against us [and did] not know what to do." In our helplessness, we fixed our eyes and fragile hopes for the life of our son on God. What else could we do?

Day after day, for three weeks, we prayed desperate prayers for Joe's life. I read my Bible and listened for God's voice like never before. I knew this was a battle only God could fight, so I put all my trust in him. I showed up at the NICU every day, all day, and in my physical, emotional, mental, and spiritual weakness, I stood firm in the strength of God. As I held Joe, I sang hymns of praise and petition, reminding God, myself, and Joe of who God is and his promises to us.

I knew Joe could die or be disabled by his illness. My prayer was for life and healing, but my hope and trust were in God and his wise will. Embracing both my reality and his sovereignty gave me strength and resolve that were not my own. In my utter weakness, I was a warrior. And God fought on our behalf.

Joe's quick and full recovery baffled his doctors. We brought him home tiny but whole. We praised God for healing Joe, and every April when his birthday comes around, I'm reminded of

God's grace to us. But even if Joe hadn't been healed, God's presence with us was the evidence of his sovereignty and love.

Everyday Battles

Life's crises level us and often leave us changed for better or for worse but for good. They are the battles that are chronicled, the epic chapters around which the stories of our lives rise and fall. They define us. But so do all the days in between.

There's a blessing in disguise that comes with our biggest trials. The circumstances are far beyond our control, our hands are tied, and so we cry out wholeheartedly to our sovereign God. Trusting in his strength to deliver us is our only option. What else can we do? But in our everyday lives, it's tempting to forget about the war and turn our trust and reliance from God to ourselves and our resources.

Second Chronicles 20 ends by telling us that the surrounding countries heard about the defeat God brought on Jehoshaphat's enemies, and the *literal* fear of God came on them.

> And the fear of God came on all the kingdoms of the countries when they heard that the LORD had fought against the enemies of Israel. So the realm of Jehoshaphat was quiet, for his God gave him rest all around. (vv. 29–30)

The result was a time of peace. During our own times of peace and rest—those times when we enjoy God's blessings with minimal trial—we need to remember the source of our strength and hope, recount and give thanks to God for his faithfulness to us in past battles fought, and prepare our hearts.

> He trains my hands for war,
>   so that my arms can bend a bow of bronze. (Ps. 18:34)

In battle, sometimes we get wounded. Our enemy uses the fear of what *may be* and the condemnation of the wounds that *have been* to enslave and blind us to the reality of the battle we are in every day. Fear and condemnation are strong taskmasters. But God can break their grasp on our hearts through the very heartache, pain, and desperate cries we so long to avoid.

As we acknowledge the reality of the spiritual battle raging around us and the calling on our lives to fight in that battle, we are both sobered and freed to stand courageously in God's might before the enemy.

As I have seen God take the things I most fear and turn what Satan means for evil to good, something has begun to happen in me. I find myself less motivated by fear and more motivated by love. And I'm going from being on the defense in the spiritual battle to taking the offense. I'm venturing into territory that before I never would have considered as I acknowledge the gifts God has given me to steward and the warrior he ordained me to be. I walk in courage and conviction and with a power that is not my own.

I wish we weren't in a war, but we are. And our certain hope is that God works all things together for our good and his glory.[11] One day, we will celebrate the final victory in heaven with Christ. Until then, may we as godly women, sisters, wives, and mothers battle courageously and equip others to do the same.

QUESTIONS FOR REFLECTION

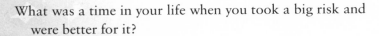
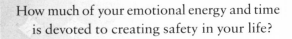

What is your greatest battle today?

How much of your emotional energy and time is devoted to creating safety in your life?

What was a time in your life when you took a big risk and were better for it?

When have you done something risky that may have looked foolish to the people in your life?

What talents are you tempted to bury in order to stay "safe"?

When you objectively consider your ambitions and efforts in a day, do they reveal an earthly or a heavenly mindset? In other words, where are you storing up your treasure?

How aware are you of the spiritual battle you are in day to day?

How does remembering the spiritual battle reframe your difficult circumstances and trials?

Do your battlefields feel more like a courtroom or a proving ground?

How has God shown up and shown off on your battlefields?

When you are in crisis, do you doubt God or recount his character and promises to him, yourself, and those around you?

What measures can you take to remember you are in a war even when things are at peace?

The Gospel's Power

Onward, Christian Lovers

"The gates of hell shall not prevail." Often quoted. More oft misunderstood.

Peter proclaims Christ, "the Son of the living God." And Christ commissions Peter, "You are Peter, and on this rock I will build my church."

Jesus calls him by his given name: "You shall be called Cephas (which means Peter)." Aramaic and Greek. The word for rock.

This is the foundation of the church. The body and bride of Christ. Built not on sand but on solid rock.

"And the gates of hell shall not prevail against it."

Look close now. Who is on the defense?

Gates barred tight. Walls built high. Inside full of huddled, fearful masses. Whispers all around.

"She marches. The body. His bride. Built on a rock. She comes with light. The truth of the despised. And he has spoken. Our gates will not hold. We shall not prevail."

The church does not hide for fear of the culture, the world, or the enemy. She has no walls, no gates to bar. She marches INTO hell. Her orders come from him who has been given "all authority in heaven and on earth." So she fears no other. She is not on the defense. She is not neutral. She is on the offense.

Her message is love.

His name is Jesus.

And demons tremble.[1]

9

Your Beautiful
"Once upon a Time"

I will reject comparison
and embrace my story.

When they measure themselves by themselves and compare themselves with themselves, they lack wisdom and behave like fools.

2 Corinthians 10:12 AMP

I'm sitting in Panera with a chai tea latte and steel cut oatmeal and thinking about you as I write. It's lunchime, but I love oatmeal. It's comforting. I'm usually here in the early morning, and now I'm noticing how different the crowd is. There are a *lot* of women here, meeting with friends, moms, and sisters. It's sweet. And intimidating. I like my morning crowd better.

To my left is one of those long tables, and in my peripheral vision I see it filling up with ladies. My music is playing in my headphones, but I still catch pieces of the conversation and laughter beside me.

"How're you doing?" one woman inquires with true compassion.

I think to myself, *How I wish someone would ask me that today.*

"I'm good. Not too much going on at work," her friend replies. You can hear the appreciation of being asked in her voice.

"Hiii-eee," another greets a newcomer in the way women do, making the one-syllable word into two (it comes out that way when you smile). Their ranks grow.

And I'm sitting here with my oatmeal. Telling you about them, feeling like an eavesdropper, and hoping no one is reading over my shoulder. And I feel *incredibly* self-conscious.

My nose won't quit itching and running, so I sniff and wipe. Did they notice? My hair wouldn't cooperate this morning. I decided I didn't care, but suddenly I do! My jeans are tight, uncomfortably so. I decided to leave my fleece workout shirt on after Pilates instead of changing into my cute bright-blue sweater. Now I regret it. And I'm eating oatmeal at 12:21 in the afternoon. What a nerd!

Yep, it's the truth.

I'm a middle-aged grandma and living a life I love, so why do I find myself thrown onto this battlefield of insecurity so often? There was a day I thought I'd overcome it, and there are many days I do. Most days I feel fairly confident and a lot less interested in, much less intimidated by, the strangers beside me. Many days I'm even happy for them and their friendships!

I've decided this battle with insecurity is consistent with humanity. Rather than feeling ashamed of the fight, I've learned to pray a simple prayer when I find myself trapped yet again in the snare of insecurity. It's this: "God, tell me who I am."

Coconut Hair

On a rare, subzero Virginia weekend in February, I was on my way to a women's retreat—the kind of event that one minute thrills you and the next fills you with dread. It promised to be a weekend of good food, deep conversations, candles, worship—and a whole bunch of beautiful women who were sure to intimidate the heck out of me. It's a strange feeling to long for something and at the same time be scared to death of it.

My good friend Tee was turning fifty and had invited the women in her life to celebrate with a weekend away at her family's beautiful waterside home. And now the day was here. As I packed, the dialogue in my head had bordered on the ridiculous and neurotic. It started with my wardrobe: I didn't have a thing to wear!

Wear what you always wear, Kim, my commonsense self said.

But none of it looks good enough, objected my inner insecurities. *My sweater is pilled. Those pants are too worn out, and that blouse isn't in style at all. Why don't I ever buy cute stuff?!*

Just pack, or you're going to be late. If it's clean, it works. Be yourself.

Myself doesn't know how to dress well. Where's Emily when I need her? How am I supposed to put together cute outfits without her? Or my sister? Why can't I dress myself?

Pack, Kim.

Finally packed and resolved to bring "myself" and my uncute outfits to the weekend retreat with a bunch of beautiful, put-together women, I jumped in the shower. I'd read recently about using coconut oil as hair conditioner and thought I'd give it a try.

We interrupt this story for a Public Service Announcement:

Do NOT try new things right before you're going to a weekend retreat with a bunch of beautiful, put-together, and likely smarter-than-you-are women.

I have slightly curly hair and am always looking for products to make it curlier. After I dried my coconut-conditioned hair with my diffuser, my curls looked great! I was so happy and feeling more confident. As I packed the car, I noticed my hair felt odd. I reached up to touch it and discovered my coconut curls were hard. Frozen hard. After a split second of confusion, I remembered that funny fact about coconut oil. It gets hard when it's cold.

With no time to redo my hair, I left the house and hoped the coconut oil would just soak in. After about thirty minutes into the ninety-minute trip, I pulled down the visor to check on my hair.

My curls weren't frozen anymore. Now they were practically flat against my head and had barely any curl to them. The warmth of the car heater was *melting* the coconut oil, and it looked like my hair hadn't been washed in a month. I panicked. Then I prayed. Except I sounded more like a woman in imminent danger of death by embarrassment and humiliation.

"GOD, HELP! I'm on my way to this retreat where the women will be beautiful, and put together, and smarter than me, and won't have coconut oil dripping from their hair!"

Then I remembered dry shampoo. I'd never used it, but it was worth a try. I pulled into a Target parking lot, ran in and bought a can, and went into one of the family bathrooms where I could try to save my swiftly sinking self-image in privacy.

It didn't work. Not even a bit.

I slinked back to my car. As I sat in the parking lot, the reality of my situation was undeniable. I would have to go to this weekend retreat where the beautiful, put-together, smart women with nice hair and intact self-images would surely take one look at me and wonder. I expected most of them would be Christians, so they probably wouldn't laugh. At least not in front of me.

I took a rubber band from my purse and pulled my greasy, coconut-infused hair back into a ponytail. I told myself I looked okay, but I felt undone.

I made my way to the retreat and tried to focus on God's goodness and truth. I knew that despite my imminent humiliation the weekend wouldn't be ruined. I'd get to shower and wash the coconut oil out of my hair forever and ever, amen. Life would go on.

The women were all I knew they'd be: beautiful, put together, smart, confident—and full of grace and kindness.

That night after a most cleansing, healing, and oil-ridding shower, I lay in bed and silently prayed: *God, why am I so un-*

done by things like this? Will I ever get over my insecurities and fear of being judged? I've come to really like how you've made me, and I feel fairly confident. I'm middle-aged *for goodness' sake! Why do I sometimes feel like I'm in junior high again?*

And this is what he told me: only *he* has the authority to tell me who I am. He drew my heart just like a daddy would pull his daughter up into his lap to comfort her and tell her again who she is: his precious daughter, the one he's proud of, the one he created, the one he adores. He showed me that while I wanted to *get over* my desire for approval, he wanted to meet it. We *need* to know who we are and that we are loved.

Our enemy and the culture are more than happy to tell us who we are. And tomorrow they'll tell us again. *Someone* will always tell us. We must decide who that will be.

If we listen to anyone (including ourselves) other than our Father, the standard will constantly change, and we will spend our lives comparing and remaking ourselves to find approval, acceptance, and love. But if we acknowledge our maker and redeemer's rightful authority to define us, we will experience the love and security that come from discovering and seeing ourselves through his design and eyes.

Where are you tempted to find your identity? In motherhood, friendships, relationships, career? Your roles will always seem bigger to you than your ability to fill them. If you seek your identity in them, you will never be enough because there is always more that can be done. Your roles are not meant to define you. The truth is not that you're too small and your role is too big; it's that your roles are too small and you're too big! *They* aren't big enough to hold your identity!

To limit your identity to a role is like saying the *Mona Lisa* is a canvas, the Taj Mahal is a building, or the Grand Canyon is a gully. While factually true, not one of those descriptions does justice to the masterpiece created by the artist who designed each work of art. Likewise, you will always be much more than a mom, wife, daughter, friend, teacher, lawyer, doctor, writer, painter.

You were created by the same One who created the universe, and you are his workmanship.

> For we are His workmanship [His own master work, a work of art], created in Christ Jesus [reborn from above—spiritually transformed, renewed, ready to be used] for good works, which God prepared [for us] beforehand [taking paths which He set], so that we would walk in them [living the good life which He prearranged and made ready for us]. (Eph. 2:10 AMP)

The Greek word that is translated "workmanship" is *poiēma*.[1] It's the word we get *poem* from. You are God's masterpiece—his poem.

A Closer Look at Me (against the Backdrop of Ps. 139 AMP-CE)

> For You did form my inward parts; You did knit me together in my mother's womb. (v. 13)

What were you thinking? I imagine an artist gathering his supplies, anticipating a new creation. Did you know what I'd look like when you were done? Or was I just a spark, a thought, a germ of an idea? But a "just" with enough hope to spur you to action. I know this feeling. It sends me to pen and paper.

"In my mother's womb." Like all human creations, made in your image, I would begin intrinsically united to another in relationship. The fruit of relationship. Three of us. Man, woman, child. Reflecting the one and three of you. Trinity.

I will confess and praise You for You are fearful and wonderful and for the awful wonder of my birth! Wonderful are Your works, and that my inner self knows right well. (v. 14)

The maker of galaxies and atoms made me. With words you commanded their existence but with hands formed mine. Such love.

My frame was not hidden from You when I was being formed in secret [and] intricately and curiously wrought [as if embroidered with various colors] (v. 15a)

Stop! I *love* that! What colors? What colors did you use to make me? You *must* have used green! Lots of it. I love your creation. The colors that come from you. *They* are intricate. The diversity of all you've made thrills my mind and calms my heart. If you made all this and constantly sustain it by your being and love me as you say you do, then I'm safe.

What else? Which other colors? What color is music? The kind that says nothing but makes me cry. And words. Knowledge. What colors are they? What color is this passion that wants to tell, to teach, to lighten the loads of others with your joy and truth?

And this. This cord that runs through the center of my being. That makes my heart beat and my body rise again, day after day. To nurture, disciple, enrich, love these ones you've given me. To watch, assess, strategize, and pray. And pray. And pray. I am the steward of an influence that will affect generations. A steward of destiny. What color is this? Deep red, I think.

in the depths of the earth [a region of darkness and mystery]. (v. 15b)

A fitting place for secrets. I forget that the Creator knows his creation better than the creation knows itself. You are the keeper of all that is true of me. The better I know you, the better I know me. Comfort.

> Your eyes saw my unformed substance, and in Your book all the days [of my life] were written before even they took shape, when as yet there were none of them. (v. 16)

Story. I love story. Setting, plot, rise, climax, resolution. Protagonist. Antagonist. Hero. In a story, they all fit perfectly together. On their own, my days, crises, joys, successes, and failures are meaningless. Futile. But in the context of story, they make sense. They have purpose. And to think it's your book! You are the author. Of my days. My life. My story. I don't need to live up to anything. I simply live. My story is perfect.

> How precious and weighty also are Your thoughts to me, O God! How vast is the sum of them! If I could count them, they would be more in number than the sand. When I awoke, [could I count to the end] I would still be with You. (vv. 17–18)

Celebration instead of Comparison

Scripture warns us against comparison.[2] If you've ever played the comparison game, you know it's a losing battle, whether you come out on top or not. We tend to compare our weaknesses to another's strengths or vice versa. I'll compare my strengths to another's weaknesses and for a moment feel a little bit better about myself—until someone stronger, faster, better comes along. On the other hand, when I "lose" at comparison, I feel disdain for myself, my "opponent," or both of us.

But when God alone gets to say who I am, I am free to look at you and *celebrate* our differences. I really like *me* a lot more, and I really like *you* a lot more. Instead of being threatened by

your strengths and saying, "You look better, dress better, and
_____ better," I am free to say, "You are beautiful! I love
that. Look at the skill God's given you." As one tiny member
of the body of Christ, I celebrate the beauty of his work in you.
Because you too are his masterful *poiēma*.

Authenticity, Diversity, and Truth

When we have acknowledged and submitted to God's authority
to define us, we are set free from the need to be like others or to
insist that others be like us. I host an annual women's retreat
called Winsome at which we intentionally make an effort to
facilitate the beautiful diversity of the body of Christ. We reach
out to and welcome speakers and attendees from diverse walks
of life, age groups, and denominations. The things we have in
common other than being women are our love for Jesus and a
deep devotion to Scripture. Beyond that, there are multitudes of
perspectives and opinions. Every year we hope that the women
who attend will be challenged and even made a little uncomfortable, because discomfort brings potential for growth.

We have three defining values that guide us: authenticity, diversity, and truth. Authenticity gives women the freedom to be
who they're created to be as well as the freedom to live in unity
with all the diverse parts of the body under the head, which
is Christ.[3] Our diversity challenges us and causes us to stretch
and grow. When we encounter perspectives that rub up against
our own, our knee-jerk reaction can be to argue or to retreat.

> In most discussions, each man has some point to maintain, and
> his object is to justify his own thesis and disprove his neighbors.
> He may have originally adopted his thesis because of some sign
> of truth in it, but his mode of supporting it is generally to block
> up every cranny in his soul at which more truth might enter.[4]

But when we learn to listen, our ideas are refined. Whether we agree or not, our perspectives are broadened. The way I see the world as a foot or ear in the body of Christ will always be unlike your perspective as a hand or eye. Learning to respect, acknowledge, and learn from the diverse perspectives of the diverse parts of the body increases our understanding and helps us to become more whole individually and corporately.

Finally, truth. Most importantly, truth. Too often, our efforts to facilitate diversity set truth aside and embrace relativism. In so doing, we pull the rug out from under any lasting purpose or meaning to our efforts. If there is no truth to be found, what is the point of honoring one another's perspectives? They don't matter.

On the other hand, if there is truth (which there must be, because even the determination of whether there is truth requires it), our collaborative and honest efforts to find truth will ultimately move us nearer to it. And *it* is him: "I am the way, and the truth, and the life" (John 14:6).

When we learn to live our stories authentically, embrace diversity, and seek truth, we are able to truly behave like a body.

The Body of Christ—the Bigger Story

My hands are one of the most appreciated parts of my body. They are extremely functional. I use them all day long. They make a way for most everything I do: eat, wash my face, shower, touch the face of my loved ones, pick things up, put things down, protect me if necessary, and so on. Without my hands, I would feel totally lost. But how foolish would it be for me to wish that all the parts of my body behaved like my hands? Besides being extremely dysfunctional, I would look like a freak. I would not be human.

186

Our bodies are infinitely diverse. We don't even have to look internally to recognize that. Even the individual parts of my hand have distinct functions, as do all my parts! My pinky toes bring balance. My eyes inform and direct my actions. My ears and mouth make communication possible.

And then there are the parts that undoubtedly have a vital function even though I don't know what it is. The second toes that are taller than my big toes. Why? My chin, knobby knees, elbows? I don't need to understand every part of my body's function to recognize its value.

My body also has scars that tell their part of my story. A C-section scar that blessed me with a pooch that will never disappear no matter how many crunches I do. It reminds me of the day a surgeon saved my youngest child's life. The many stretch marks across my belly and hips testify to six living, breathing souls that began in my womb.

The way my body works is masterful. How much more can we see this in the body of Christ? Paul's description in 1 Corinthians 12 sheds much light on the importance of acknowledging and appreciating both our function and our purpose and those of others. It is a rich and directive analogy. As we look at this illuminating passage, I want to highlight three things: (1) examples of comparison, (2) God's sovereignty and purpose in design, and (3) the role of the weak.

> For just as the body is one and has many members, and all the members of the body, though many, are one body, so it is with Christ. For in one Spirit we were all baptized into one body—Jews or Greeks, slaves or free—and all were made to drink of one Spirit.
>
> For the body does not consist of one member but of many. If the foot should say, "Because I am not a hand, I do not belong to the body," that would not make it any less a part of the body.

And if the ear should say, "Because I am not an eye, I do not belong to the body," that would not make it any less a part of the body. If the whole body were an eye, where would be the sense of hearing? If the whole body were an ear, where would be the sense of smell? (1 Cor. 12:12–17)

The first example of comparison says that because I'm not like you, I don't measure up or belong. The foot says, "Because I am not a hand, I do not belong to the body." And the ear says, "Because I am not an eye, I do not belong to the body." Paul refutes this absurdity by stating the obvious: each part has its necessary function.

"But as it is, God arranged the members in the body, each one of them, as he chose" (v. 18). Each member's place in the body is not random. God has intentionally composed the body with purpose. That means he's placed you where he wants you with the function he intended. It also means that the parts of the body he has specifically connected you to are significant in your life as well. *Every* part of the body is integral to the other, but there's no denying that my fingers and hand have a unique and intimate relationship. Acknowledging and embracing the places you are connected—the people he has placed in your life—is essential to fulfilling your purpose as a member of the body.

If all were a single member, where would the body be? As it is, there are many parts, yet one body.

The eye cannot say to the hand, "I have no need of you," nor again the head to the feet, "I have no need of you." (vv. 19–21)

The second example of comparison says that because you're not like me, you aren't necessary. "I have no need of you." It's that quiet, arrogant thing we do when we dismiss someone who, for whatever reason, we don't esteem.

> On the contrary, the parts of the body that seem to be weaker are indispensable, and on those parts of the body that we think less honorable we bestow the greater honor, and our unpresentable parts are treated with greater modesty, which our more presentable parts do not require. (vv. 22–24a)

God's upside-down kingdom in which the last and least are first shows up in his body. Those we would deem weak and unnecessary Paul tells us are "indispensable." Note he doesn't admonish us to be nice and accepting and smile and say hello. "The parts of the body that seem to be weaker" are to be given "greater honor" and treated with "greater modesty." The idea is that we intentionally take measures to acknowledge, honor, care for, and protect the "weak."

> But God has so composed the body, giving greater honor to the part that lacked it, that there may be no division in the body, but that the members may have the same care for one another. If one member suffers, all suffer together; if one member is honored, all rejoice together.
> Now you are the body of Christ and individually members of it. (vv. 24b–27)

Notice God's intent in his composition of the body. The honor given to the body's weaker members is for the purpose of avoiding division and unifying the body as all its members suffer, honor, and rejoice together as one.

The more we consider the analogy of the body, the more we learn about God's perspective of his people. While he calls us his children, we know a body is even more unified than a family. I care deeply for my loved ones and their pain and hurts, but the pain I experience in my own body is recognized immediately. If there's something off in one member of my body, all my parts know it right away. If my body is healthy, all the parts immediately begin to work together to bring relief to the part that is suffering. The weaker and more vulnerable parts of my body are cared for by the rest. Our entire skeletal system is designed to protect our brain, eyes, lungs, vital organs, and more. My body literally *cannot* survive without the other parts. And not even the tiniest member of the body can function without being connected to my brain, the head.

Apply all of this to us as the body of Christ, and we get a glimpse of how integral we are to one another, the way the weaker members are actually the most vital to the church, and how every member must be connected to Christ, the head of the body.

But if this chapter is about embracing *my* story, why so much talk of the body and others? Our stories are more accurately defined as chapters in *the* grand story of the gospel. Far from being a separate novel still awaiting positive reviews, your story is integral to the message of the gospel.

Lesson from a Little Girl

It was late, and I was alone in the auditorium helping to clean up and prepare the room for the morning session. Here I was at yet another women's retreat. What is it about women's retreats that is so irresistible to me, a woman who finds women intimidating at best and terrifying at worst?

I know I'm not alone. We are hardwired for community. After all, we are made to be parts of a body! Our longing for love is universal. When women are at their best, they're experts at loving and encouraging one another. But most of us have seen that same powerful influence used to tear down rather than build up, and we can become gun-shy.

Some of us become expert at wearing masks. We take the pulse of a community and adapt chameleon-style. We find a tenuous acceptance at too high a price. Others simply withdraw. The game is too fierce and not worth the blood and bruises. Either way, we all miss out on the power of life-giving, God-honoring, empowering friendship.

As I straightened chairs and pondered my convoluted female relationships, I was startled by the memory of her face. She was in fourth grade and always the first to welcome the new girl.

"Hi! My name's Kim. What's your name?"

She was me. Me before I'd felt the sting of gossip. Before I'd been laughed at and left to eat lunch alone. Before I'd become the unsuspecting subject of notes passed back and forth—words penciled sharp on scraps of paper that cut invisible wounds. It would have hurt less had you stabbed me with the pencil. She was me before I'd been ambushed by the frenzied hornet nest of females on the hunt.

Call them mean girls. Call it bullying. The terminology wasn't around then, and it wouldn't have mattered if it was. Women of every age can be brutal. Our power to nurture, heal, encourage, and bring growth can morph into something that can slice a sister's jugular vein with a look and leave her bleeding out with no remorse. I know. I've been on both sides of that sword.

Her smile, eager eyes, and voice took me back. I remembered the joy and excitement. The freedom!

I want to restore that in you.

It wasn't audible, but it was unmistakable. It was my Father's voice.

"What do you want to restore, God?"

Her fearlessness. Her passion. Her joy and desire to offer her friendship to another.

"I'm not so sure about that. Too risky."

This *is too heavy. Weighing, analyzing, allowing the wind of a look or a word said or not said to determine your course.* "Do

191

they like me? Am I being too friendly? Not friendly enough? Do I fit in?" Or that other mode you try when the first one exhausts you: "Forget it. I don't need them." It's a losing game even when you're "winning." A desperate, disordered dance. It's not how I made you.

"Okay. If you say so. But I'm gonna need you to tell me who I am. A lot."

Of course. Don't be afraid, my precious daughter. Remember, I have rescued you. I have called you by name, and you are mine. I will be with you and will protect you. You are precious in my eyes. I love you.[5]

Embracing My Story

We love stories because they're different. I've read many books in my lifetime, and I've enjoyed them all because they're different. They have different plots, different focuses, different perspectives, different trials. When I begin to embrace my story, I can appreciate the differences and that mine doesn't look like yours.

But when I compare my story against another, I not only dishonor the author but also diminish the purpose and beauty of my story. Comparison wants to level the field and narrow the qualifications and insist that *these* traits are the only desirable ones. It doesn't allow for diversity, growth, maturity, strength, and weakness.

We also appreciate stories that have *all* the elements needed for a good story: protagonist, antagonist, rise and fall, climax, resolution, conflict, and so on. If we could write our own stories they would probably be flatlines; we wouldn't choose the trials or villains. But a flatline isn't a story. It's dead.

Embracing my story in its entirety—the good and bad, the beautiful and ugly, the blessed chapters and broken ones—frees me to fulfill my purpose and live the rest of the chapters with freedom and joy. My story isn't defined by its worst page or even chapter. My story is perfect for *me*.

Your story might involve all sorts of trials I could never fathom, or it may be full of chapters that are like fields rich and full. I want to be able to read your story and give thanks to a good God instead of comparing.

As my story has unfolded, I've been tempted to question God's timing. There are chapters I would like to rewrite, but then I remember *who* the author is. I'm learning to trust and find contentment, and I'm coming to love my story with all its successes and mistakes, joys and sorrows, trophies and scars.

My story isn't over. It's still being told. It's had dark chapters and brilliantly light ones. I'm hoping for more of the latter, but I know pain is as inevitable as joy. Not only will I experience my own pain, but the more people I love, the more I will encounter pain as they walk through difficult times. Our loved ones carry our hearts around wherever they wander.

Your story isn't over either. Prince Charming may not come. Even worse, he might leave. Our children will disappoint and may even devastate us. Not every dream will come true, and some will surprise us beyond any dream we could have ever imagined. We don't have a promise that our stories will turn out the way *we'd* like them to. But if our confidence and hope are in Christ, our stories, just like their author, are perfect.

Maybe the best part of our stories is that they don't end.

QUESTIONS FOR REFLECTION

Is it difficult or easy to embrace your story? Why?

How have you allowed culture to tell you who you are?

Based on Scripture, who does God say you are?

Based on what you know about yourself, how has God uniquely designed you?

What are practical ways you can overcome comparison with celebration?

How might valuing authenticity, diversity, and truth enrich your story and relationships?

How have you experienced being strengthened by the body of Christ?

How can you engage in a deeper way with the body of Christ?

What parts of your story might God want to restore?

Heavenly Minded

*I will reject myopic, earthbound plans
and embrace grand, eternal destinies.*

Has this world been so kind to you that you should leave with regret? There are better things ahead than any we leave behind.

C. S. Lewis[1]

M om's end came fast. Her cancer diagnosis had come less than a year before, and now we were gathered with family and friends waiting with her in my parents' living room. Waiting for death.

Hospice care is an odd thing. I'm sure generations before saw death and the nearness of it as normal. But to our Western world with all its hospitals and hideouts, bringing a soul into her home—the very center of her home—well, it just seems strange. And I was afraid.

My dad's call came just ten days before we said good-bye. He asked me and my sister to come. We each threw whatever we thought we'd need in our bags, I drove to Missy's house, and we were on the road within hours. We joked later that Missy had packed enough clothes for both of us to take a cruise, and I had enough books for us to read nonstop for a month. We were new at this.

And now a week later, we found ourselves in the middle of the strangest mix of sorrow, reunion, laughter, heartbreak, fear, and peace. This was death up closer than we'd ever seen it before, and it was intimidating. We rearranged furniture in the living room to accommodate Mom's hospital bed, made dozens of calls, learned about saying good-bye from nurses and social workers, and even met with funeral directors *before* Mom was gone—a necessary task no one likes to talk about.

But there was a profound sense of hope as well. The house was overwhelmed with food that comforted our bodies and weary hearts almost as much as the kind souls who delivered it.

We became hosts. As friends arrived, we helped them become comfortable with the foreboding shadow that had settled in the living room right beside Mom's bed. Then we introduced them to this newfound and unexpected visitor—hope.

As we gathered around, praying and singing Mom's favorite hymns, I was struck by how many of the familiar songs speak of heaven in their last verse. Although I'd heard these hymns most of my life, I'd never heard these *heavenly* verses.

The hope and sure confidence in these words moved me. They sounded as if those who'd penned them knew what they were talking about, and they helped me not to be afraid.

> Then shall my latest breath whisper Thy praise;
> This be the parting cry my heart shall raise;
> This still its prayer shall be,
> More love, O Christ, to Thee,
> More love to Thee, more love to Thee!
> > Elizabeth P. Prentiss, "More Love to Thee"

> Let goods and kindred go,
> This mortal life also;
> The body they may kill:
> God's truth abideth still;
> His Kingdom is forever.
> > Martin Luther,
> > "A Mighty Fortress
> > Is Our God"

> While I draw this fleeting breath,
> When my eyelids close in death,
> When I soar to worlds unknown,
> See Thee on Thy judgment throne,
> Rock of Ages, cleft for me,
> Let me hide myself in Thee.
> > Augustus M. Toplady,
> > "Rock of Ages"

Then in a nobler, sweeter song,
I'll sing Thy power to save,
When this poor lisping, stammering tongue
Lies silent in the grave.
    William Cowper, "There Is a Fountain"

And when my task on earth is done,
When, by Thy grace, the victory's won,
E'en death's cold wave I will not flee,
Since God through Jordan leadeth me.
    Joseph H. Gilmore, "He Leadeth Me"

When was the last time you heard a sermon about death that wasn't at a funeral? I'm not sure why we've become so estranged from heaven, but I believe living with the sober reality of both our mortality *and* the hope of eternity has the potential to fill our lives on earth with purpose, freedom, and joy!

Nearsighted Faith

I think perhaps the reason we're so prone to neglect thoughts of eternity and heaven is because we've become spiritually near-sighted. Our hearts, and therefore our ambitions and plans, have ceased to see beyond what's right in front of our short lives.

myopia—nearsightedness; lack of foresight or discernment[2]
myopic—nearsighted; shortsighted[3]

The glasses prescription for spiritual myopia is a submitted and humble heart. We put them on, and everything comes into focus. Our knowledge of this universe testifies to the glory of a brilliant Creator God. The large and small joys of life begin to instruct us in the ways of love. Our best efforts and even our worst failures serve to demonstrate our need for someone beyond ourselves to help us live good lives. And most importantly, we know *this* isn't all there is.

Heavenly Minded

There's an old saying, "Some people are so heavenly minded that they are of no earthly good." It's not meant to be a compliment. It arouses images of prissy piety and harsh judgment. Someone who spends so much time in religious pursuit that they're obnoxiously ignorant of the "real world." Maybe you've known someone like this. Sadly, the reputation of the body of Christ has been marred and often unfairly judged based on just such a person. There's no question that "faith without works is dead" (James 2:20 NKJV). We must give more than lip service to the gospel.

But *not* to be heavenly minded is by default to be earthly minded. It's one or the other. If we reject an eternal and heavenly perspective of success and purpose, we will embrace this world's perspective, and our actions will follow. Fame, numbers, wealth, people's approval, and so on will define the effectiveness of our efforts.

A popular quote by C. S. Lewis tells us, "Aim at Heaven and you will get earth 'thrown in': aim at earth and you will get neither." But what precedes it both informs the quote and gives us a practical understanding of what it means to be truly heavenly minded.

A continual looking forward to the eternal world is not (as some modern people think) a form of escapism or wishful thinking, but one of the things a Christian is *meant to do*. It does not mean that we are to leave the present world as it is. If you read history you will find that the Christians who did most for the present world were just those who thought most of the next. The Apostles themselves, who set on foot the conversion of the Roman Empire, the great

200

men who built up the Middle Ages, the English Evangelicals who abolished the Slave Trade, *all left their mark on Earth, precisely because their minds were occupied with Heaven.* It is since Christians have largely ceased to think of the other world that they have become so ineffective in this. Aim at Heaven and you will get earth 'thrown in': aim at earth and you will get neither.[4]

Thirty Years

As we drove onto the campus of my alma mater, I had that disorienting feeling you get when you know you've been here before but hardly anything looks the same. I searched for familiar landmarks, but they were hidden among larger, newer buildings and even newer construction. Joe directed us to his dorm. These were my old stomping grounds, but my son knew his way around better than I did. We went around the circle and something began to feel familiar.

"Take your next right," Joe said.

Jeff complied, and then I saw it.

"That's my dorm! Number 27!"

It looked just the same! I toned down my enthusiasm, not wanting to rob Joe of his exciting new college experience with his mom's trip down memory lane. But when we pulled up to Joe's dorm, just two buildings over from his dear old mom's, and walked in, I couldn't help myself. The halls still looked the same. The pay phones had been replaced, but other than that (and the fact that we were in a male dorm) it was the fall of 1985! I could practically see the big hair and hear Amy Grant and Carmen in the halls (it was a Christian university). I held my tongue, as the memories poured from their vaults like a flood.

The next couple days were spent getting Joe settled and exploring the new face of my old campus. Since Jeff and I had gotten married while I was still in school, the town held many memories as well. We found some of our old haunts and continued to be amazed by all the memories.

We were also humbled as we considered God's love and faithfulness through all that had happened in our lives over the last thirty years. *Was it really thirty years ago?*

As we drove away from town, my mind began to wander toward the future and the next thirty years. What might *they* look like? And then came the sobering thought, *Would there be another thirty years to look back on one day?* When we started our journey, we naively took the future decades for granted, but now we know better. While we plan to be around as long as we can, we've sat in too many hospital waiting rooms, attended too many funerals, and said good-bye to too many people to know *for sure* that we have three decades still ahead of us. And just in case we forget the reality of our mortality, our bodies are happy to remind us. These days they demand more attention, are pickier about what we eat and what we lift, and generally require less abuse and more rest. There's no denying the finiteness of our days on this earth.

> So teach us to number our days
> that we may get a heart of wisdom. (Ps. 90:12)

We don't know if we'll even have tomorrow. Living with this reality isn't morbid; it's wise. And it focuses our minds and hearts on what we have been promised—eternity with God in heaven.

Fixed

In a world full of distractions and a life full of trials that demand our immediate attention, how are we to keep a heavenly mindset? I believe the answer is simple and hard at the same time. Here's the simple part: "fixing our eyes on Jesus, the author and perfecter of faith" (Heb. 12:2 NASB). The hard part is figuring out how to keep this eternal focus.

In the Christian classic *Your God Is Too Small*, author J. B. Phillips asserts just that—our culture's estimation of God is too small.

> It is obviously impossible for an adult to worship the conception of God that exists in the mind of a child of Sunday-school age, unless he is prepared to deny his own experience of life. If, by a great effort of will, he does do this he will always be secretly afraid lest some new truth may expose the juvenility of his faith. And it will always be by such an effort that he either worships or serves a God who is really too small to command his adult loyalty and cooperation.[5]

Phillips goes on to explain how a "god" like this is unsatisfactory to a thinking culture.

> Many men and women today are living, often with inner dissatisfaction, without any faith in God at all. This is not because they are particularly wicked or selfish or, as the old-fashioned would say, "godless," but because they have not found with their adult minds a God big enough to "account for" life, big enough to "fit in with" the new scientific age, big enough to command their highest admiration and respect, and consequently their willing cooperation.[6]

Clearly, this is *not* the God of the Bible. But our efforts to make God relatable often make him too much like us. We are in danger of losing our awe with regard to the incarnation of God in Christ. Because we are no longer amazed, our estimations and expectations of God have shrunk. Timothy Keller describes this "minimizing" of God in his book *Hidden Christmas*:

In Jesus the ineffable, unapproachable God becomes a human being who can be known and loved. And, through faith, we can know this love. This does not stun us as much as it should.[7]

Keller then tells of hearing a conference speaker describe the majesty of Creator God:

If the distance between the Earth and the sun—ninety-three million miles—was no more than the thickness of a sheet of paper, then the distance from the Earth to the nearest star would be a stack of papers seventy feet high; the diameter of the Milky Way would be a stack of paper over three hundred miles high. Keep in mind that there are more galaxies in the universe than we can number. There are more, it seems, than dust specks in the air or grains of sand on the seashores. Now, if Jesus Christ holds all this together with just a word of his power (Heb. 1:3)—is he the kind of person you ask into your life to be your assistant?[8]

God is hardly an *assistant*. The author of Hebrews tells us "our God is a consuming fire."

Therefore, let us be grateful for receiving a kingdom that cannot be shaken, and thus let us offer to God acceptable worship, with reverence and awe, for our God is a consuming fire. (Heb. 12:28–29)

Reverence. Awe. Keller writes:

Anytime anyone drew near to God it was completely terrifying. God appears to Abraham as a smoking furnace, to Israel as a pillar of fire, to Job as a hurricane or tornado. When Moses asked to see the face of God, he was told it would kill him, that at best he could only get near God's outskirts, his "back" (Exod. 33:18–23). When Moses came down off the mountain, his face was so bright with radiance that the people could not look at him (Exod. 34:29–30)—so great, so high and unapproachable is God.[9]

Protocol

The invitation came on official United States Naval Academy stationery. I could tell right away that this was something special, not like the other mail we'd received as parents of a midshipman. It was an invitation to an awards banquet for finalists in an ethics department essay competition. I remembered Josh briefly mentioning something about an essay he'd written and his professor's request to enter it. It seemed he'd done well.

I was extremely proud of Josh's attendance at the Naval Academy. Any mom would be, but when you homeschool there's something especially affirming about your child's accomplishments. I'll be the first to confess to vicarious feelings of success! But I was superintimidated by the academy. They had a protocol for *everything*—where to walk, how to speak, who to speak to. Even though very little of this protocol applied to civilians, every time we visited Josh on the yard (USNA talk for campus), I felt nervous.

As the day of the banquet drew near, I checked and rechecked the invitation for time, dress, and details. The dress was business casual. Finally, the big day came. Jeff and I had taken our kids to his family's river house for a few days and had just enough time to get home, freshen up, and get back on the road for the hour drive to the academy. Now something you need to know is that Jeff and I are *very* casual dressers. So when I read "business casual," I thought his short-sleeve, collared shirt, khakis, and five o'clock shadow and my almost miniskirt, beach hair, and dressy slides would be just fine.

About twenty minutes into our trip, I remembered how detailed military protocol can be and almost panicked. "What if 'business casual' means something different in the military than it does in the civilian world?!" Sure enough, I googled *military civilian dress protocol* and up came a detailed dress chart for civilians attending military functions. We did *not* pass muster. Jeff was missing the required blazer, and I could only imagine his five o'clock shadow wasn't up to code either. And my skirt was certainly too mini, my hair too beachy, and my slides too—well, just not right at all.

We considered stopping and making some quick clothing purchases, but it would make us late. I wrestled with my imminent embarrassment for a while but then decided we'd just try to sit near the back where we wouldn't stand out.

When we finally arrived, Josh greeted us and led us to the table to check in. The woman manning the table found our name tags, smiled, and said "Congratulations!" Josh introduced us to a couple more people as we entered the ballroom and looked for a seat in back. They also congratulated us.

"Josh, why are these people congratulating us?" I asked.

Josh smiled like a Cheshire cat. "Because I won the essay contest. Surprise!"

I was so proud and excited for both Josh and me. Another homeschool mom notch!

"And we are sitting at the Naval Academy superintendent's table!" said Josh.

My excitement and pride turned to quiet panic. So much for being inconspicuous.

Sure enough, we sat at the superintendent's table. In the front of the room. And stood in front of the entire ballroom with Josh and the superintendent for pictures when he was given his award.

We survived, but it was an epic protocol failure.

Holy

As my story illustrates, protocol is still alive and well in the military. It's worth considering why. Ultimately, the military retains protocol because it knows what is on the line—security, freedom, life, and death. *Yes, sir. No, sir. This is how/what/when we do, sir.* These simple responses reflect an understanding not only of protocol but also of rank, authority, and power, all necessary for security.

Culturally, we aren't much for protocol. It seems stuffy and meaningless. We celebrate our freedom and dare anyone to tell us how we should dress, talk, or live our lives. Maybe in part our cultural distaste is understandable. When protocol becomes detached from what it represents—its meaning—and only serves people's pride, it becomes useless. On the other hand, protocol can serve as a powerful reminder of vital truths.

Protocol is found throughout Scripture. God's perfect holiness requires perfect righteousness. In order to approach him, one must be pure. The Jewish priests who represented the people before God would purify themselves before they entered the Holy of Holies. Even then, they would enter with bells and ropes tied around their ankles. If the bells went silent, the people would know that the priest had died before the presence of God, and they would drag him out with the rope.

Let's sit with that a moment. It's not the image of God we're accustomed to hearing about. Remember Hebrews 12:29? "Let us offer to God acceptable worship, with reverence and awe, for our God is a consuming fire." As Keller reminded us, this is the God whose presence would kill even Moses, the man he himself had chosen.

Where religious pride has usurped meaningful traditions meant to symbolize and remind us of the unseen spiritual world, religious protocol loses its meaning. However, when in our modernity we dismiss tradition and protocol from our worship, we risk losing the awe and reverent fear of a holy God.

Jesus gave us the sacrament of communion to continually remind us of our sin and his holiness. When we receive communion, we have the opportunity to be awed once again by the perfect righteousness of God even as we are embraced by his love and grace in our imperfection. "For our sake he made him to be sin who knew no sin, so that in him we might become the righteousness of God" (2 Cor. 5:21).

Sin. *This* is the intersection where a perfect God meets our imperfect lives. The perfect fellowship of Eden is restored. Our inescapable imperfection paves the way for remembrance. At the foot of the cross that was necessary because of my sin, I am reminded of this great Creator God incarnated in flesh that drips the blood by which I'm cleansed. His perfect holiness and love inspire awe, reverence, intimacy, and joy.

It's here, in the face of sin and death, where eternity begins to take hold of my heart and mind. And at an empty tomb, my eternal security is sealed.

Grand, Eternal Destinies

We must embrace the reality of our *eternal* lives and live with a long view of today. This switch in perspective has the power to take us from a life consumed with what we can see and know and cram into one short, frustrated lifetime to a life lived out of the potential to affect eternity every single day. Living with eternity in mind puts our temporal lives on earth into perspective and gives us the vision we need to live courageously as strangers on our journey home.[10] It causes me to realize my actions today have eternal implications and to live like it.

When my life is consumed with myopic (shortsighted) earth-bound plans and I fail to look to what's eternal, I accept only the gifts that I call good. But when I take off the blinders and look with spiritual eyes, I can see the beauty in what otherwise I would consider bad. I can see hope in things that without Christ would crush me. I can see how he uses the trials and circumstances of my life to create eternal peace. And I can look at my loved ones and see beyond the challenges right in front of me.

I have to take the blinders off every day. Some days I forget and see only my and others' failures and shortcomings. But when I remember we are created for eternity, I can see the potential and opportunity in conflicts. I can see the gospel's relevance in the struggles. I'm okay with not knowing and waiting on God. Because if he's willing to work out his good will for all eternity, then I can take the struggle, trial, and heartache. When my heart embraces this hope, I can grasp why there is trial, and James's instructions to *rejoice* when trials come make sense.[11]

If it was just about the here and now—my comfort on this earth and building my *own* kingdom—life's struggles would be the antithesis of my heart's goals. But when I look at the cross and God's kingdom, I know I could be a failure in the world's eyes but a heroine in his.

It's ironic. Keeping both our mortality and our eternity in focus actually brings a deeper sense of purpose to our living days. It frees us from the deceptive traps of living for temporary things—the kinds of things that don't matter once we die. And it opens the doors to courageous choices, dreams, and pursuits that will live long after we have relocated from this world to the next. As Lewis said, our *heavenly* mindedness will enable us to leave our mark on this world.

God has a grand, eternal destiny for each of us. He has written an amazing story. No one ever before or ever after will have your story. May God give us eyes of faith and hope so that we can look at our days, weeks, months, and years with an eternal perspective.

> I am the resurrection and the life. Whoever believes in me, though he die, yet shall he live, and everyone who lives and believes in me shall never die. Do you believe this?
>
> Jesus (John 11:25–26)

QUESTIONS FOR REFLECTION

How much do you think about heaven? Is doing so uncomfortable or hopeful? Why?

In your experience, how would you describe the connection between humility and a proper perspective of God?

How do you think being *heavenly minded* can increase your influence for good on earth?

How do you think numbering our days makes us wise?

What practical things can you do to keep focused on Jesus?

How has religious protocol and tradition influenced your faith for good or bad?

What inspires reverence and awe of God in you?

How might embracing an eternal perspective encourage you in your life on earth?

Acknowledgments

Having never written a book before, I have nothing literary to compare this process to. But as a mother who has brought six living, breathing souls into this world, birth is something I'm somewhat familiar with. And writing this book is much like conception, gestation, and delivery. One woman may bear all the signs of something being born, but countless others invisibly come alongside the process of new life. So it is with words.

These words were conceived in my heart and home, and no one deserves more acknowledgment and thanks than you, Jeff. You've pushed me out the door literally and figuratively for over three decades. When I wanted to hide, you convinced me there was too much wonderful waiting for me. You were right, and I'd never have known it without your belief and support. Your fingerprints are all over my heart and, therefore, these pages. Thank you. You're my favorite.

Josh, Daniel, Emily, Ben, Joe, and Sam, your love and grace for your *very* imperfect mama are testaments to the grace, love, and forgiveness of our generous Father. You are my children, but you're also my teachers. Most importantly, you are my brothers and sister eternally in Christ. Words fall far too short to express my gratitude for each one of you. You truly are my reward, and I love you.

Emily, your story is integral to mine and much of it is told here. Thank you for sharing it so bravely and letting me do the same. You might be my daughter, but your courage inspires and instructs your mama. Of the many incredible women I know, you are one of those whom I most admire.

Kim, Hilary, Ethan, and Margaret, you were the faceless ones I imagined and prayed for as I dreamed of what "happily ever after" might be for Josh, Daniel, Emily, and Ben. Thank you for loving and adding so much to our family.

Amelia, Elisha, and Ezra—oh, how your mina loves you! May you three precious souls and all who come after truly know that "the Lord your God is God, the faithful God who keeps covenant and steadfast love with those who love him and keep his commandments, to a thousand generations" (Deut. 7:9).

Mom and Dad, your love for me and for words formed my heart. Your persevering love for each other taught me to fight for love and family. And your love for God taught me my life's purpose. Thank you. Even though you're apart for a while, your love still grows.

Missy Pratt, no one knows you quite like a sister. I'm so happy to have shared so much life with you. Your love and enthusiasm for people and God are beautiful. Thank you for loving me so well, making me laugh, encouraging women beside me, and cheering me on. You're my favorite sister.

Stephanie Avellino, God knew I'd need you. I'm so glad he made us traveling partners. Marriage, motherhood, and ministry are less scary and so much more doable with your constant love and friendship. Thank you, friend.

Angie Gyovai, you come in and out of my life but always leave me more loved and affirmed. All those years (of diapers and strollers) ago, you listened to my journal entries and told me one day I'd write a book. Thank you for your steadfast friendship and belief in my words. They have kept me moving forward more times than you know.

Debbie Morgans, thank you for living and loving so bravely and generously. Your persevering faith has made you a powerful healer. Thank you for letting me share your story of sorrow and grace and the way it has formed me as a mom.

Tee Kelly, you ask the best questions and are the queen of hospitality. Though it's not as often as I'd like, time with you always feeds my soul and spirit with the sweetest sustenance. Thank you for sharing the beauty of your home and giving me a quiet place to hide and write.

To the women who first heard this message taught—thank you for sharing your lives and stories. Watching the message of God's grace bring you freedom gave me passion and courage to keep sharing.

Winsome leadership team (past and present) and dear friends— Julie Dodson, René White, Natalie Joy, Wendy Bracken, Donna Christophersen, Maeve Gerboth, and Clare Ruysen (and Emily, Hilary, Margaret, Missy, Steph, Debbie, and Tee)—thank you for believing in Winsome and helping to make it happen. I treasure your friendship and support.

Thank you to every woman who has bravely joined us at Winsome each spring. Your stories have encouraged and challenged me to keep showing up, and it's a privilege to walk and learn with you. Your authenticity, gorgeous diversity, and truth-seeking ways inspire me continually.

Nicol Epple, you're one of those people I met online and then met up with in real life—just like we tell our kids to never do! I'm so glad we did. You're crazy courageous, and I'm so grateful to walk this adventurous road of ministry beside you.

Jennifer Hand, your friendship and prayers have carried me so many times. Thank you for always being just a *vox* away. Your love for God and submission to his Spirit make you mighty, friend. Glory!

To the many women who have written and walked beside me—my friendship with most of you was born online and grew in this world of words, and now we're sisters. You have each been instrumental in my writing journey, and I'm so grateful for you.

Emily Wierenga, your generous encouragement at the beginning of my "public" writing gave me courage and introduced me to the beauty and richness of online community. Thank you!

Holley Gerth, your God-sized dream gave birth to the team and launched me into the scary steps ahead. Thank you for caring so much about women and sharing your friendship, encouragement, and knowledge so generously.

Deidra Riggs, you took a chance on me at JTreat, and this book came of that. You are one of the most courageous and authentic women I know, and I'm grateful to be your friend.

Ann Kroeker, you're part fairy godmother, part midwife, and have become *all* trusted friend. Thank you for holding my hand, pushing and cheering, and guiding me and my words with your expert knowledge and insight. Your coaching has been one of the best investments I've ever made in myself both personally and professionally.

Fellowship Bible Church Pastors Mark Carey and Don Den Hartog, thank you for your insight and encouraging feedback on my manuscript. Your leadership and love for God and his Word have provided our family with a place to grow in the grace and knowledge of Jesus.

Rebekah Guzman, thank you for attending my breakout session and asking for my proposal . . . and then patiently waiting a year. You were a wonderful surprise gift from God, and your confidence in this message has inspired mine. Thank you for seeing the potential it has to bring freedom to women.

Jamie Chavez, thank you for your expert, thorough, and patient instruction. Your humor has made one of the scariest parts of this endeavor fun! I'm grateful to have worked with an editor of your caliber on my first book.

To everyone at Baker Books who has had a part in bringing this message to print—what an honor it is to work and advance God's kingdom with you! Thank you.

To every person who whispered a prayer, sent a note, or shared a word of encouragement as I wrote—thank you.

Finally and always, God. You made yourself real to me when I was still a child, and your steadfast love and presence have been my salvation. Your perfection no longer scares me but beckons me to your grace. May my life and words always bring the message of your great gospel.

Notes

Chapter 1 The Gospel, a Perfect Fit for Your Reality

1. *Dictionary.com*, s.v. "perfectionism," accessed January 15, 2017, http://www.dictionary.com/browse/perfectionism.

2. *Blue Letter Bible*, s.v. "menō" (Strong's no. G3306), https://www.blueletter bible.org//lang/lexicon/lexicon.cfm?Strongs=G3306&t=KJV.

3. R. C. Sproul, ed., *New Geneva Study Bible* (Nashville: Thomas Nelson, 1995), 1694.

4. Elyse Fitzpatrick, *Counsel from the Cross: Connecting Broken People to the Love of Christ* (Wheaton: Crossway, 2012), 24.

Chapter 2 Humility's Good Fruit

1. *Dictionary.com*, s.v. "perfectionism."

2. See Isa. 55:9.

3. Rick Warren, *The Purpose Driven Life* (Grand Rapids: Zondervan, 2002), 148.

4. *Dictionary.com*, s.v. "perfectionism."

Chapter 3 Guilty? Yes. Condemned? No Way!

1. *Blue Letter Bible*, s.v. "katakrima" (Strong's no. G2631), https://www.blue letterbible.org//lang/lexicon/lexicon.cfm?Strongs=G2631&t=KJV.

2. Sproul, *New Geneva Study Bible*, 1987.

Chapter 4 *That* Peace

1. Ralph Waldo Emerson, "The Over-Soul," in *Essays: First Series*, 1841.

Chapter 5 His Sovereignty, My Security

1. James D. Bratt, ed., *Abraham Kuyper: A Centennial Reader* (Grand Rapids: Eerdmans, 1998), 488.

2. Gal. 5:1 and 2 Thess. 2:15.

3. Sproul, *New Geneva Study Bible*, 1883, 1888.
4. Eph. 1:11.
5. Jerry Bridges's book *Trusting God* is a great starting point for the topic of God's sovereignty.
6. Isa. 55:9 and Rom. 11:33–36.
7. Prov. 25:2.
8. *Blue Letter Bible*, s.v. "heautou" (Strong's no. G1438), https://www.blue letterbible.org/lang/lexicon/lexicon.cfm?Strongs=G1438&t=KJV.
9. Gen. 50:20.
10. Exod. 3:14.
11. Rom. 8:22–23.

Chapter 6 Ideal or Idol?

1. Gen. 29–31.
2. Exod. 32.
3. Exod. 12:35–36.
4. Rom. 12:1 (NKJV and AMP).
5. Ps. 18:30 and Isa. 55:8–9.

Chapter 7 Liar, Liar, Pants on Fire

1. William Berry, "The Truth Will Not Set You Free," *Psychology Today*, May 6, 2012, https://www.psychologytoday.com/blog/the-second-noble-truth/201205/the-truth-will-not-set-you-free.
2. For a detailed exposition of truth and its spiritual, intellectual, and cultural ramifications, I highly recommend Nancy Pearcey's books *Total Truth*, *Saving Leonardo*, and *Finding Truth*.
3. Ps. 30:5.
4. Rom. 5:3–5.
5. 2 Cor. 5:7.
6. James 3:18.
7. Richard Chenevix Trench, "Human Experience, Different Minds," in Bliss Carman et al., eds., *The Higher Life*, vol. 4 of *The World's Best Poetry*, 1904, http://www.bartleby.com/360/4/172.html.
8. Sproul, *New Geneva Study Bible*, 1510.
9. Sproul, *New Geneva Study Bible*, 1515.
10. Matt. 6:25–33.
11. Ps. 139:17–18.
12. Col. 3:3.

Chapter 8 Women in Combat Boots

1. Ann Voskamp, *The Broken Way: A Daring Path into the Abundant Life* (Grand Rapids: Zondervan, 2016), 138.
2. Sproul, *New Geneva Study Bible*, 1548.
3. Eph. 6:17.
4. Found in Eph. 6:14–18 and worth studying, remembering, and applying daily.

5. 2 Cor. 12:9.
6. Rom. 7:24–8:4; also see chap. 3 above.
7. Ps. 139:16; Eph. 1:11; and Job 42:2.
8. Judg. 7:1–8.
9. *Blue Letter Bible*, s.v. "paniym" (Strong's no. H6440), https://www.blueletter bible.org//lang/lexicon/lexicon.cfm?Strongs=H6440&t=KJV.
10. 2 Chron. 20:7–11.
11. Rom. 8:28.

Part 4 The Gospel's Power

1. Matt. 16:18; John 1:42; Matt. 28:18; and James 2:19.

Chapter 9 Your Beautiful "Once upon a Time"

1. *Blue Letter Bible*, s.v. "poiēma" (Strong's no. G4161), https://www.blueletter bible.org//lang/lexicon/lexicon.cfm?Strongs=G4161&t=KJV.
2. 2 Cor. 10:12.
3. Col. 1:18.
4. George MacDonald, *The Curate's Awakening*, ed. Michael R. Phillips (Minneapolis: Bethany, 1985), 158.
5. Isa. 43:1–2, 4.

Chapter 10 Heavenly Minded

1. C. S. Lewis, *Letters to an American Lady*, reissue ed. (Grand Rapids: Eerdmans, 2014), 124.
2. *Dictionary.com*, s.v. "myopia," accessed January 16, 2017, http://www .dictionary.com/browse/myopia.
3. *Dictionary.com*, s.v. "myopic," accessed January 16, 2017, http://www .dictionary.com/browse/myopic.
4. C. S. Lewis, *Mere Christianity*, vol. 1 of *Mere Christianity and The Screwtape Letters* (New York: HarperCollins, 2001), 134, emphasis added.
5. J. B. Phillips, *Your God Is Too Small* (New York: Macmillan, 1961), 7.
6. Phillips, *Your God Is Too Small*, 8.
7. Timothy Keller, *Hidden Christmas* (New York: Viking, 2016), 53.
8. Keller, *Hidden Christmas*, 53.
9. Keller, *Hidden Christmas*, 53–54.
10. 1 Pet. 2:11.
11. James 1:2.

Kim Hyland is a writer, a speaker, and the founder and host of Winsome, an annual retreat for women that celebrates authenticity, diversity, and truth. She also speaks at national retreats and conferences, where she encourages women by sharing her imperfect path and God's perfect plans. Originally from the DC metro area, she now lives with her family on a mountain overlooking the Shenandoah Valley in Virginia. Connect with Kim at WinsomeLiving.com.

CONNECT WITH KIM!

Photo credit: Purple Fern Photography

To learn more about Kim's writing and speaking, visit **WinsomeLiving.com**.

For information about the Winsome Retreat, visit **WinsomeRetreat.com**.

LIKE THIS
BOOK?
Consider sharing it with others!

- Share or mention the book on your social media platforms. Use the hashtag **#AnImperfectWoman**.

- Write a book review on your blog or on a retailer site.

- Pick up a copy for friends, family, or anyone who you think would enjoy and be challenged by its message.

- Share this message on **FACEBOOK** and **TWITTER**:
  "I loved #AnImperfectWoman by @WinsomeWoman // WinsomeLiving.com @ReadBakerBooks"

- Share this message on **INSTAGRAM**:
  "I loved #AnImperfectWoman by @KimHyland // WinsomeLiving.com @ReadBakerBooks"

- Recommend this book for your church, workplace, book club, or class.

- Follow Baker Books on social media and tell us what you like.

  f Facebook.com/ReadBakerBooks

  🐦 @ReadBakerBooks